MW01489556

This is a work of narrative nonfiction and dramatized history. While based on real people and events, certain conversations, scenes, and internal monologues have been interpreted or fictionalized for narrative cohesion. Every effort has been made to remain faithful to the historical record as presented in primary source materials.

For information about permission to reproduce portions of this work, or to inquire about adaptation or licensing rights, please contact: Spectorcreative.com

The Time of Clive: The Battle that Shaped an Empire

Written by Scott Neitlich
Cover design by the Shawn Justin.
Maps and illustrations by the author.

Published by Amazon Kindle on Demand

ISBN: 97982833386138
Printed in the United States of America

First Edition: April 2025

123456789

'

Dedicated to Brian King and Greg Miller for all the real-life Indiana Jones adventures we shared exploring the "lost Delta of India".

At Disneyland.

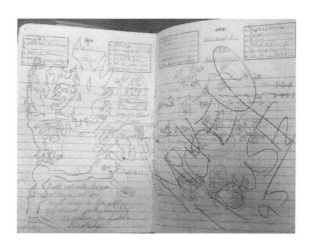

Also, by the Author (*or coming soon!*)

INSTRUCTIONAL:

Doodling with Purpose: Hieroglyphs for the Modern Student

GRAPHIC NOVEL:

Myth Wars Vol 1: Zeus the Teenage Years

HISTORICAL NONFICTION: '

The Nile Quest: The Victorian Race to Uncover the Greatest Secret of the Ancient World

Columbus' Secret Mission: How Columbus hid his Jewish Heritage and his Quest for the Lost Tribes

The Dinosaur War: Revenge, Ruin, and the Race for the First Fossil Bones

Revenge of the Wolf: The Forgotten Admiral Who Shaped the Modern World

Fall of the West: The Epic Battle for Constantinople that Changed the World

Operation: MIDDLE EARTH. The Forgotten 1838 U.S. Military Mission to Reach Hollow Earth

The Time of Clive: The Battle that Shaped an Empire

VISUASLIZED CLASSICS:

Moby Dick by Herman Melville – *Visualized Edition*

The Time of Clive
The Battle that Built an Empire

By Scott D. Neitlich

Robert Clive AKA Clive of India

Forward: "Why is this guy Clive and why should I care?"

It all started with Indiana Jones.

Not in a lecture hall or a dusty library, but in a darkened movie theater sometime in the early 1980s. I was a kid then—wide-eyed, sugar-charged, gripping a tub of popcorn too big for my lap. I didn't know much about history. I certainly didn't know anything about colonial India. But I knew adventure when I saw it. And *Indiana Jones and the Temple of Doom* was pure, unfiltered adventure. Rope bridges, mine carts, secret cults, and the immortal line: "Fortune and glory, kid."

But one line stuck out, even then. A throwaway line, almost buried in the noise: "The British never forget the mutiny of 1857."

I didn't know what it meant. Not really. But it lingered.

Years later, rewatching the film as an adult, another line leapt out—this time from Indiana himself: "Back in the time of Clive..." Again, a single sentence. No explanation.

Just tossed out with the casual authority that Harrison Ford brought to every role. Yet something about it grabbed me.

Who was Clive? Why did his "time" matter? And what, exactly, had happened in 1857 that the British never forgot?

As a kid, *Temple of Doom* was just a ride. As an adult, it became a map—full of hidden passages leading to questions I'd never thought to ask.

And so I followed them.

Not with a whip and fedora, but with books. With articles.

With dusty maps and contradictory records and a lot of late-night internet deep dives. I discovered that "the time of Clive" wasn't just a nod to some British general. It was a reference to Robert Clive—Clive of India, as he was later called—an Englishman who, through a mixture of ambition, military brilliance, and ruthless manipulation, laid the foundation for the British Empire in the East.

And that discovery led me to the Battle of Plassey.

Plassey, like Clive himself, is a name that's unfamiliar to most Americans. We don't teach it in our schools. It rarely features in our history books. Ask an American student about the American Revolution or the Civil War, and they'll give you a paragraph. Ask them about Plassey, and you'll get a shrug.

But here's the thing: Plassey changed everything.

On a humid morning in 1757, in a mango grove in Bengal, a small force of British East India Company soldiers faced off against a massive army commanded by the Nawab of Bengal, Siraj ud-Daulah. Outnumbered more than ten to one, the British had no business winning.

And yet, they did.

Because Robert Clive had done more than bring muskets and cannon. He had brought contracts. He had brought promises. He had brought betrayal. And in doing so, he didn't just win a battle—he reshaped the map of the world.

The British East India Company was not a nation. It had no crown, no anthem, no flag recognizable to anyone outside the docks of London. It was, essentially, a corporation. And yet after Plassey, it became something more. With the Nawab defeated and a puppet ruler installed, the Company controlled Bengal—and from there, began its slow and brutal expansion across the subcontinent.

What followed was nearly two centuries of British rule in India. Rule by company. Rule by crown. Rule by decree. And, eventually, resistance. From the rebellion of 1857 (yes, the very mutiny Indiana Jones offhandedly referenced), to the nonviolent campaigns of Mahatma Gandhi, to the final declaration of independence in 1947, the echoes of Plassey rippled outward across centuries.

All because of one morning in one orchard.

The more I read, the more astonished I became—not just at the magnitude of what Clive had done, but at how little attention we give it today in the West. Here was a story with all the elements of legend: betrayal, ambition, colonialism, commerce, courage, and cruelty. And yet, it was reduced to a sentence. A throwaway line.

"The time of Clive."

So I decided to tell the story the way it deserved to be told.

Not as a textbook. Not as a dry, academic analysis. But as an adventure.

Because that's what it was.

That's what it still is.

This book is part of a larger series I've been developing—true histories told in the tone of an epic. They are meant to read like the films that inspired me, but they are rooted in rigorous research and a respect for the past. History should be gripping. It should have weight. It should remind us that the people who shaped the world weren't statues—they were men and women who made choices, gambled, failed, succeeded, and lived in shades of gray.

Clive was not a hero.

Nor was he merely a villain.

He was, like all great historical figures, complicated. Daring. Strategic. Arrogant. Haunted. A man who believed he could shape the world—and did.

In writing *The Time of Clive*, I wanted to capture that complexity. I wanted readers to feel the humidity of Bengal, to hear the roar of cannon fire at Plassey, to taste the ink of secret treaties and bribes disguised as honor. I wanted to explore how an empire could be built not just by armies, but by accountants. By signatures. By moments of silence where one man does nothing—and in doing so, changes everything.

That's the thing about history—it's not just about what happened, but about what we choose to remember.

In American schools, we're taught a lot about the Founding Fathers, the Civil War, the World Wars. We memorize dates, names, and places that shaped our own national identity. But we're rarely encouraged to explore the events that defined *other* nations—especially when those events were driven by economic conquest or colonial exploitation in which our own ancestors may have been bystanders, beneficiaries, or unwitting participants.

Growing up, I never heard of the East India Company. If it came up at all, it was in vague terms—like a sort of British Amazon or proto-corporate trading guild. But that description doesn't do justice to what the Company became. After Plassey, it functioned like a private government. It had its own army, its own taxes, its own prisons and judges. At its height, it controlled more people than any European monarchy. And yet it was never voted into office. Never elected. Never truly accountable.

It was born from trade.

And trade—when backed by guns—became empire.

Robert Clive didn't just defeat an enemy general. He helped rewrite the rules of modern geopolitics. His victory at Plassey allowed a private company to install a puppet ruler, loot a treasury, and then extract wealth from one of the richest regions on Earth for decades. Bengal wasn't some far-off outpost. It was the crown jewel of Mughal India, home to art, literature, philosophy, and a flourishing textile industry that rivaled anything in Europe. And after 1757, it began to unravel under the pressures of colonial exploitation.

Famine came. Not just from drought—but from policy. Taxes were levied on grain in the midst of crop failure. Local industries were gutted to serve the Company's export needs. Revenue collectors operated like warlords. Some historians estimate that the Bengal Famine of 1770 killed more than ten million people.

Let me repeat that: ten million.

And this wasn't an unintended consequence of war. It was the price of profit.

That fact haunted me the deeper I went.

Because it challenged the way I'd been taught to think about progress, about capitalism, about "civilization." Clive and the Company didn't set out to exterminate people. But their systems were designed to extract wealth, not support life. The consequences were catastrophic.

And yet... Clive is still remembered, in many British sources, as a kind of genius. He's praised for his military brilliance, his daring strategy, his empire-building savvy. And yes, he was all of those things. But at what cost?

What happens when you win everything, but lose your soul?

Clive himself struggled with that question. After his return to England, he was celebrated as a hero, given titles and estates. But the accusations of corruption, of excess, followed him. He defended himself before Parliament with the now-famous line: *"I stand astonished at my own moderation."*

But he wasn't moderate. He was meticulous. And the toll of that weighed heavily on him.

He died by suicide in 1774.

By then, the Company was entrenched, and the cycle had begun. More conquests. More "reforms." More famines. Eventually, the abuses became so untenable that even the British government stepped in to take direct control of India in 1858—just one year after the massive, bloody uprising we now call the Sepoy Mutiny (and which Indian historians rightly call the First War of Independence).

And here, again, I return to that line in *Temple of Doom*—"The British never forget the mutiny of 1857."

That wasn't just a line to add texture. It was a nod to a real trauma in British imperial memory. The uprising terrified the colonial establishment. It was brutally suppressed, and afterward, British rule became more direct, more rigid, more racialized. The Company faded into history, but the structure it had created lived on—until finally, after nearly two centuries, Gandhi and the independence movement dismantled it.

But it all started with Clive.

And that realization hit me hard.

Because we're so used to thinking of history as compartmental-ized: American history, European history, Asian history. But these are false boundaries. What happened in Plassey reshaped global trade. It helped finance British industrialization. It af-fected the flow of cotton, of labor, of military focus. It rippled across oceans and decades.

And yet we're not taught it.

It's not on the test.

Unless you go looking for it, you won't find it.

Which is why I wrote this book.

I wanted to bring it back into the light—not just for students or history buffs, but for anyone who's ever wondered how we got here. Why certain nations became powerful. Why others were impoverished. Why the scars of empire still shape our headlines today.

I also wanted to show that history doesn't have to be boring.

It can be thrilling.

It can have cliffhangers and betrayals and long shadows cast by cannon smoke.

I wrote *The Time of Clive* in the style of the old adventure novels and films that first sparked my curiosity. But every scene is grounded in real events. Every character is drawn from history. I didn't invent the drama. I just unearthed it. Clive's story is stranger than fiction—and far more consequential.

And as I wrote, I kept thinking of young me, sitting in that theater, hearing that line:

"Back in the time of Clive…"

This book is my answer to that line.

It's a journey back to that time. To that place. To the moment the modern world began to shift—not with an election or an invention, but with a bribe, a cannon, and the silence of a man who chose to wait rather than fight.

To those just discovering this history, I hope this book offers a thrilling, sobering, and necessary perspective. To those who already know it—especially readers from South Asia, for whom these events are not academic but ancestral—I hope

I've done justice to the gravity of what was lost, what was endured, and what was ultimately reclaimed.

Because history isn't just about who won.

It's about who remembers.

And now, hopefully, more of us will.

—Scott Neitlich
Greensboro NC, 2025

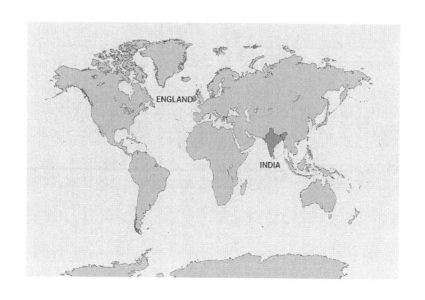

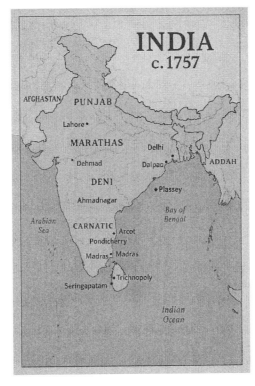

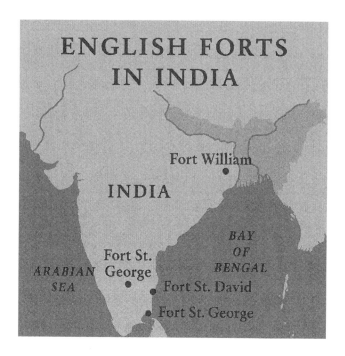

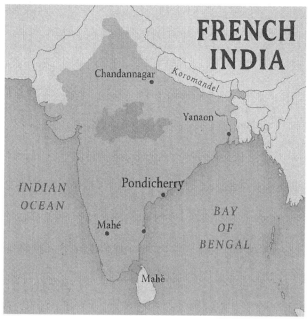

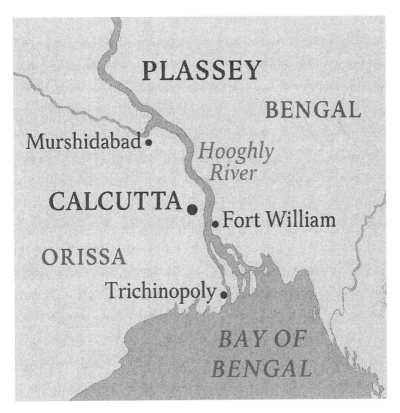

PLASSEY

BENGAL

Murshidabad

Hooghly River

CALCUTTA

Fort William

ORISSA

Trichinopoly

BAY OF BENGAL

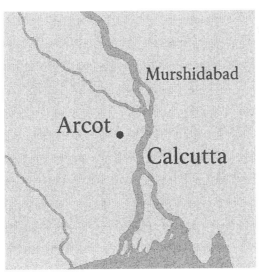

Murshidabad

Arcot

Calcutta

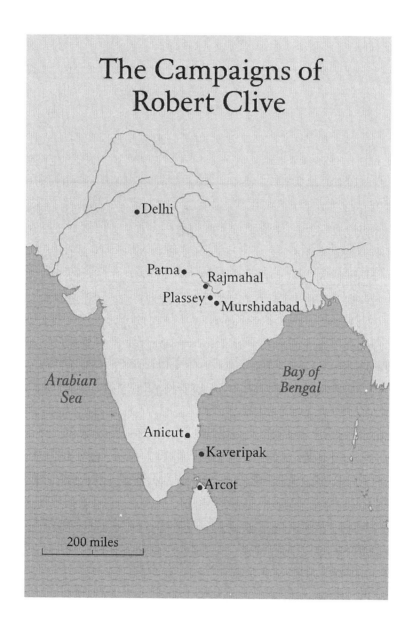

Siraj ud-Daulah

Introduction: The Road to Plassey

To understand why the Battle of Plassey changed the course of world history, one must first understand why it happened at all.

Plassey was not just a clash of armies—it was the result of a perfect storm of imperial ambition, economic desperation, fractured sovereignty, and opportunistic betrayal. Set in Bengal, one of the richest provinces of Mughal India, the battle was fought between a small British East India Company force led by Robert Clive and the vast army of Siraj ud-Daulah, the Nawab of Bengal. Behind both stood powerful forces—on one side, the growing commercial-military apparatus of the British Empire; on the other, the fracturing remnants of an ancient empire and the interests of European rivals.

Geography and Wealth of Bengal

In the mid-18th century, Bengal was not a remote outpost—it was the economic heart of India. Fertile, densely populated, and home to a thriving textile industry, Bengal generated enormous wealth through rice, silk, cotton, and opium. The Hooghly River, a distributary of the Ganges, made Calcutta a vital hub of trade. Whoever controlled Bengal's treasury and its ports controlled the flow of wealth across the subcontinent—and from there, into Europe.

The Decline of the Mughals and Rise of Regional Nawabs

For centuries, India had been under the rule of the Mughal Empire, a dynasty of Muslim emperors who governed over a multiethnic, multicultural society with a blend of administrative skill and military might. But by the early 1700s, the empire was fracturing. Local rulers—nawabs, rajas, and marathas—

began asserting their autonomy, collecting taxes, raising armies, and negotiating their own treaties with foreign powers.

In Bengal, the position of Nawab had become semi-independent. While still nominally under the Mughal emperor, the Nawab functioned as a sovereign ruler. By 1756, that ruler was Siraj ud-Daulah—a young, impulsive, and often erratic leader who inherited not just a throne but an increasingly tense political landscape.

The British East India Company

The British East India Company, chartered in 1600, was originally a merchant venture seeking to profit from trade in spices, cotton, and tea. But by the 1700s, it had become something more: a quasi-state with its own army, navy, and diplomatic service. The Company had been expanding its presence in India for over a century, establishing fortified trading posts in Bombay, Madras, and Calcutta.

By the mid-18th century, the Company was facing mounting pressures. Competition with other European powers—especially France—threatened its profits. The cost of maintaining garrisons, forts, and administrative offices drained its resources. The directors in London demanded results: secure trade routes, loyal local rulers, and a reduction in French influence. Military conquest was not yet official policy—but it was becoming a tempting tool.

The French East India Company

France, too, had its own East India Company, based out of the southern city of Pondicherry. Though smaller in scale, it had made strategic alliances with local Indian powers and successfully challenged the British in several skirmishes. In the Carnatic Wars (1744–1763), French and British forces fought proxy battles across southern India, often supporting rival Indian princes to extend their influence.

In Bengal, the French were less entrenched but nonetheless viewed by the British as a serious threat. Intelligence suggested that French agents were courting Siraj ud-Daulah and encouraging him to act against the British.

Siraj ud-Daulah's Position

When Siraj took the throne in 1756, he was immediately faced with internal dissent. The court was divided. Powerful bankers like Jagat Seth and generals like Mir Jafar questioned his legitimacy and worried about his volatility. At the same time, Siraj feared—and resented—the growing military presence of the British and French in Bengal.

In June 1756, Siraj acted decisively. He marched on Calcutta and seized Fort William, the British stronghold in the city. Many British soldiers and civilians died, some reportedly in the infamous "Black Hole of Calcutta" incident, where dozens of prisoners suffocated in an overcrowded cell. While the historical accuracy of this account is debated, the effect in Britain was explosive.

The British Response: Enter Clive

The East India Company could not afford to lose Calcutta—not just for financial reasons, but for prestige. They dispatched Robert Clive, already a veteran of campaigns in southern India, to lead a retaliatory expedition.

Clive was not a typical soldier. He had once been a Company clerk. But through a combination of charisma, boldness, and brutal strategic thinking, he had risen to command. Upon retaking Calcutta in early 1757, Clive quickly realized that military victory alone wouldn't secure Bengal. He needed a political solution.

That solution was Mir Jafar.

The Conspiracy

Mir Jafar, one of Siraj's top generals, had long been dissatisfied with the Nawab's rule. Clive, along with Company agents and the powerful banker Jagat Seth, conspired to replace Siraj with Jafar. In exchange, Jafar would guarantee favorable terms for British trade and reimburse the Company for the cost of the campaign.

The plan was sealed in secret correspondence.

At the same time, the French were offering Siraj support, but hesitantly—Paris had not authorized full military engagement. Siraj, caught between factions and not knowing who to trust, prepared his army for battle.

He had over 50,000 men.

Clive had 3,000.

But Clive had something Siraj didn't: silence. Jafar's men would not fight.

The Battle of Plassey

On June 23, 1757, the two armies met near a mango grove outside the village of Palashi—rendered in British accounts as "Plassey." What followed was not a heroic clash of arms, but a masterstroke of manipulation. As Siraj's troops advanced, Jafar's division stood still. Clive's disciplined forces, supported by superior artillery and coordinated volleys from sepoys, broke the Nawab's center. Within hours, the battle was over.

Siraj fled. He was captured and killed shortly thereafter.

Jafar was installed as Nawab.

The Company took control of Bengal's treasury.

The Aftermath: The Beginning of Empire

The victory at Plassey was far more than a military win. It was the moment the East India Company became a territorial power. With Bengal under its thumb, the Company controlled not only a vast economic engine, but also the political machinery that would allow it to expand further across the subcontinent.

This expansion came with consequences.

The Company imposed tax systems that prioritized remittance to London over the welfare of Indian farmers. The textile industry, once the envy of the world, was hollowed out. A series of famines—most notably in 1770—claimed millions of lives.

Indian governance structures were co-opted, manipulated, or dismantled. And behind it all was the silent, enduring consequence of Plassey.

French-British Rivalry Beyond Bengal

The Battle of Plassey must also be seen in the broader context of European rivalry. The British and French East India Companies were not merely trading rivals; they were political instruments of their respective monarchies, and by the mid-18th century, their confrontations in India mirrored the wars being fought across Europe and the Atlantic.

The War of the Austrian Succession (1740–1748) and the Seven Years' War (1756–1763) turned India into a theater of global conflict. In southern India, the Carnatic Wars pitted British and French-backed Indian princes against one another. In these battles, men like Clive learned not just how to fight, but how to exploit India's internal divisions. Forts changed hands. Towns were looted. Alliances were formed and discarded.

Although the French held key enclaves such as Pondicherry and Chandernagore, their strategic posture was weakened by limited naval support and slower decision-making from Paris. When Siraj ud-Daulah sought aid in 1757, the French were hesitant. Their local commander, Law, provided some support, but not enough to alter the outcome. This hesitation gave the British an opening—not just militarily, but diplomatically.

The rivalry reached its climax after Plassey. While the British consolidated Bengal, the French presence began to erode. By the end of the Seven Years' War, France had lost most of its influence in India. Plassey didn't just mark the fall of Siraj—it marked the end of French ambition on the subcontinent.

The Economics of Extraction and the Bengal Famine

With Bengal under its control, the East India Company did not waste time. Its primary goal was profit. Through a system of tax farming, Company officials outsourced revenue collection to local intermediaries who were incentivized to extract as much wealth as possible. The logic was simple: maximize returns for shareholders in London.

This model gutted the local economy.

Traditional industries, especially textiles, were upended. Bengal had once exported high-quality muslin and silk to markets across Asia and Europe. Now, the Company restructured trade to prioritize raw materials like indigo, opium, and saltpeter. Artisan communities were devastated.
Some were forced into indenture or abandoned their trades entirely.

The most catastrophic consequence came in 1770.

After years of economic extraction, the region was hit by a drought. Crops failed. But the taxes did not stop. The Company refused to reduce its demands. Granaries were emptied.

Peasants died in the millions. In some districts, one-third of the population perished. Contemporary accounts describe rivers clogged with corpses, whole villages abandoned, and children sold for a handful of rice.

It was one of the deadliest famines in recorded history—and it was not a natural disaster. It was a policy failure.

Empire, Identity, and the Philosophical Divide

Underlying the military and economic dimensions of Plassey was a deeper cultural rift. The British and their European contemporaries operated from a worldview shaped by Enlightenment rationalism, mercantile capitalism, and an emerging belief in racial and civilizational superiority. Many saw India not as an equal civilization, but as a decadent empire in decline—one ripe for intervention.

Indian rulers, on the other hand, governed through a framework that blended Mughal administrative traditions, Islamic jurisprudence, Hindu dharma, and local customs. Power was distributed across a mosaic of religious, ethnic, and regional identities. For centuries, this system had allowed India to sustain both unity and diversity.

But it was not designed to resist an external force with a singular focus on profit.

Where Indian sovereignty emphasized patronage, land grants, and social cohesion, the Company emphasized quarterly revenue. Where Indian courts dealt in ritual, alliance, and negotiation, the Company imposed ledgers and legalese.

Plassey marked the moment these two systems collided—and one began to overwrite the other.

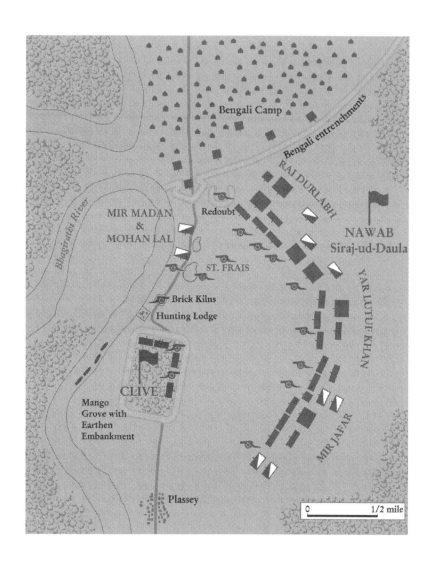

Bengali Camp

Bengali entrenchments

RAI DURLABH

Redoubt

MIR MADAN
&
MOHAN LAL

NAWAB
Siraj-ud-Daula

ST. FRAIS

YAR LUTUF KHAN

Brick Kilns

Hunting Lodge

CLIVE

Mango
Grove with
Earthen
Embankment

MIR JAFAR

Bhagirathi River

Plassey

0   1/2 mile

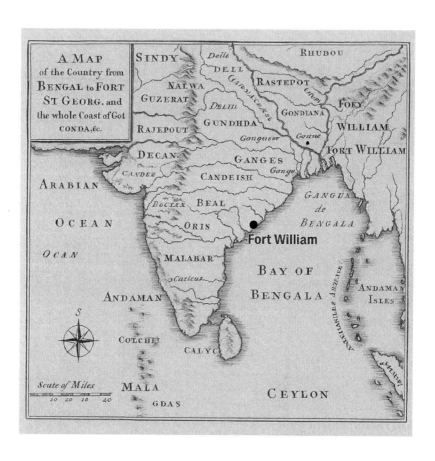

Fort William

Prologue Part 1: The Black Hole of Calcutta

June 20, 1756 – Calcutta, Bengal

The air was thick with rot and gunpowder. Mosquitoes danced like ash in the dying light as the British flag sputtered on its pole above Fort William. Below, inside the ramparts, the remnants of the garrison gathered in silence—sweat-soaked, bloodied, and defeated.

The fort had never truly been finished. Built in haste and arrogance, it was a British creation thrust into the heart of Bengal not for war, but for commerce. It had wide halls for ledgers, armories meant more for show than siege, and officers who measured success not in victories, but in cargo tonnage. But war had come anyway. And now, the Nawab of Bengal, Siraj ud-Daulah, stood at the gates.

The British hadn't expected him to move so fast—or so ruthlessly. Days earlier, his forces had descended on Calcutta with the fury of betrayal. The East India Company had fortified their position without his consent. They had ignored his writ, defied his taxes, and provided sanctuary to enemies of his court. And when he responded, they had underestimated him.

Now, the British defenders—barely more than a hundred soldiers, merchants, and civilians—had lost the fight.
Roger Drake, the acting governor of Calcutta, had already fled by boat under cover of darkness, abandoning the fort to its fate. The native sepoys had deserted in waves. Only a skeleton crew remained, led by the young and unlucky John Zephaniah Holwell, a Company administrator turned reluctant commander.

Holwell gripped the wall's parapet with trembling hands, eyes fixed on the smoke curling above the city beyond. Screams still echoed in the distance—of looting, of vengeance, of a city turned over to chaos. He had ordered the white flag raised at dusk, but the silence on the Nawab's end unnerved him.
And then, the gates opened.

A thunder of boots. A ripple through the defenders. Holwell turned just in time to see Siraj's men pour into the courtyard— infantry in bright silks, elephants adorned in armor and bells, and, riding behind them, the young Nawab himself. He was barely twenty, face painted in kohl, robes flowing like a storm cloud.

He dismounted slowly. Deliberately. He said nothing for a long time.

Then he spoke in clipped Persian through an interpreter.

"You have insulted Bengal."

Holwell stepped forward, stiffly. "We surrender, Your Highness. The fort and its people are yours."
Siraj said nothing. His gaze wandered across the assembled prisoners. Europeans, mostly. A few Indians loyal to the Company. Some too wounded to stand. Others hiding their fear behind coats and cravats stained with blood.

"You will be held," the Nawab said at last. "Until your punishment is decided."

He turned and left.

Holwell breathed out slowly. Alive, at least. That was something.

But as the sun dipped behind the eastern palisade, the nightmare truly began.

The guards pushed them in with the butts of their muskets.

It was a small room—stone-walled, windowless, once used for storing munitions, perhaps. No more than 18 feet by 14, with a single iron-barred vent near the top of the far wall. By Holwell's count, 146 people were forced into the space. The door clanged shut behind them with finality.

At first, there was murmuring. Then shouting. Then the first cries.

The heat hit like a furnace. With no ventilation, no water, and no room to sit or move, bodies pressed against each other in a heaving mass of panic. Some pounded on the walls. Others clawed at the vent. The air turned fetid in minutes. Breathing became a chore. Fists flew. A woman screamed. A man dropped to his knees, sobbing, "My God, my God…"

Holwell tried to climb toward the barred vent, using the mass of bodies as a makeshift staircase. He reached it—briefly—and gasped in the cooler air. "Take turns!" he called. "Pass it along!

There's air here!"

But reason dissolved as quickly as the night deepened. Thirst set in like madness. The sweat of dozens pooled on the floor, slick and warm. People collapsed. Some were trampled. Others were crushed against the wall. The youngest suffocated first.

At some point, Holwell passed out.

He awoke hours later—if time meant anything anymore— wedged between two corpses, his face pressed to the back of a man whose shirt was soaked with blood. His mouth was too dry to scream.

A woman in the corner tore at her gown, trying to breathe.
Another man tried to bite through his own wrist.
One of the guards outside opened a slot in the door and peered
in. He wrinkled his nose.

"There is no space for mercy," he said.

Then the slot shut.

By morning, 123 people were dead.

When the door finally opened—slowly, as if reluctant to dis-
turb the tomb—only 23 staggered out alive. Holwell among
them, though barely.

He didn't speak at first. Just stared. A clerk tried to wrap a
bandage around his shoulder, but he brushed the man away.

The others were silent too. The survivors were ghosts.
Siraj had not intended for them to die, or so the court historians later insisted. The order had been for imprisonment, not
slaughter. But the guards had interpreted their duties literally.

Or sadistically. Or both.

The British, however, would not forget. Nor would they for
give.

What followed in the official East India Company dispatches—penned by Holwell himself—was a tale of atrocity,
elevated to myth.

"The Black Hole of Calcutta," the Company called it.

The name stuck. It spread through London like a fire, igniting
the newspapers and fueling outrage.

By the time Robert Clive read the first account, he was already preparing for war.

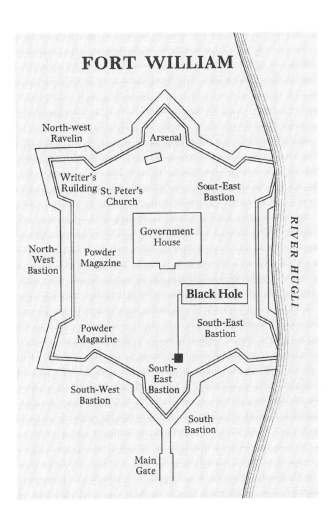

Prologue Part 2: March on Bengal

Madras Presidency – July 1756

The first time Robert Clive read the account, he didn't flinch.

He held the parchment steady, eyes scanning each line as the words bled horror: "crushed by the mass," "heat unimaginable," "screams into silence." The description of Holwell's ordeal in the "Black Hole" was vivid and calculated—perfect for outrage, and perfect for vengeance.

Clive finished reading, then folded the document with precision. He stood from his desk and looked out over the barracks of Fort St. George. A humid wind blew in from the coast, carrying the scent of gunpowder and salt.

He turned to his aide-de-camp. "Summon the Council. At once."

The aide nodded and ran.

Clive stood in silence a moment longer. Not because he was shocked—but because he wasn't. India was a land of cruelty and opportunity in equal measure, and Clive had known both.

But this? This was a gift.

Because war in India wasn't declared from London. It was made here, in places like Madras and Calcutta. And if the Company wanted vengeance—if England wanted a story to stir the blood of Parliament—he would give them one.

He would retake Bengal. He would crush Siraj ud-Daulah. And he would never let the British forget who had done it.

The council met that night under a canopy of flickering lanterns and rising heat.

Governor Pigot of Madras presided, sweating through his coat.

The senior merchants and officers surrounded him—fat with trade wealth, thick with powdered wigs and powdered arrogance. Clive sat at the edge, leaning forward like a wolf among sheep.

Pigot cleared his throat. "We have received the official account from Mr. Holwell in Bengal. The Nawab of Bengal has taken Fort William. The loss of life, as you have seen, is appalling. The Company expects a response."

A murmur ran around the table. Some spoke of diplomacy.

Others urged delay until reinforcements arrived from London. One even suggested bribes.

Clive stood.

"Gentlemen," he said, voice clipped, deliberate. "There is only one appropriate response."

They turned to him—some curious, others wary. He was, after all, not one of them. Clive was not born into wealth. He had clawed his way here.

He continued. "We must take Bengal back. Not simply Calcutta—Bengal itself. The Nawab believes the Company is weak. He must be shown he is wrong."

Pigot tapped the table. "And how exactly would you do this,

Mr. Clive? March north through jungle and swamp with a handful of men? Bengal is not Arcot."

Clive's lips curled into a ghost of a smile.

"I've done more with less."

The plan was audacious.

Clive would take a force of 900 European infantry, 1,500 sepoys, eight field guns, and a handful of artillery officers. They would embark by sea up the Bay of Bengal and land near the Hooghly River. From there, they would march upriver toward Calcutta—through monsoon-fed jungle, hostile territory, and with no guarantee of native support.

It was a suicide mission. Or a masterstroke.

But Clive had two weapons better than muskets: *surprise* and *reputation*.

He spent the next two weeks assembling the force. Rations were packed. Gunpowder was loaded. Sepoys were drilled until their feet blistered. The Company's merchants protested the cost. Clive ignored them.

His men didn't love him. But they feared him. That was enough.

They boarded the transport ships in early August, sails unfurling against a bruised sky. The monsoon had not yet broken, but the sea boiled in anticipation.

As the ships pulled away from Madras, Clive stood on the deck of the *Tyger*, eyes fixed on the horizon. He said nothing.

But in his coat pocket, folded and reread a dozen times, was

Holwell's letter.

"They died gasping."

He would not let them die in vain.

They made landfall near Falta, south of Calcutta, in late December. The jungle loomed behind them, the river to their left, and the Nawab's spies already moving in the trees.

Clive wasted no time. Scouts were sent upriver. Supply lines were secured with brutal efficiency. He bribed local zamindars and intimidated the rest. And every night, he held counsel with Admiral Watson of the Royal Navy, who had accompanied the expedition with several war sloops.

"We must hit them before they entrench," Clive said, leaning over a map.

Watson nodded. "And if they've already entrenched?"
Clive looked up.

"Then we dig them out."

By early January 1757, Clive stood once more on the muddy outskirts of Calcutta, now guarded by a token force of Siraj's troops—underpaid, undertrained, and unprepared for what was coming.

Clive gave the order.

The assault was swift and ferocious. British cannon fire shredded the eastern wall. Sepoys surged forward, bayonets fixed.

The defenders broke within an hour. Calcutta fell back into Company hands.

But Clive wasn't done.

He marched straight into Fort William, straight to the site of the Black Hole. It had already been swept clean. The blood scrubbed from the stone. The cell left dark, empty, and echoing.

He stepped inside alone.

The door shut behind him.

He stood in the silence, imagining it: the screams, the bodies, the clawing hands.

Then he whispered into the dark.

"Not again."

End of Prologue

Clive at 19.

Chapter 1: The Suicide That Did Not Take

Robert Clive did not belong.

Not in the manicured fields of Shropshire, not in the cloistered classrooms of Market Drayton Grammar School, and certainly not among the genteel sons of merchants who dressed like lords and recited Horace as if the world depended on it. He was born in 1725 in the small market town of Styche, the son of a modestly placed squire, a lawyer of no note and even less warmth. The Clive family was respectable but unremarkable—landed, yes, but hardly aristocracy.

Young Robert was a problem almost from the start.

He was unruly, combative, and brilliant in all the wrong ways.

He climbed rooftops to frighten townsfolk. He fought every boy who looked at him the wrong way—and a few who didn't.

He organized a gang of older boys to extort pocket change from shopkeepers under the pretense of "protection." When one shop refused, Clive sat outside for hours with a sling, shattering windows until the man relented.

Teachers despaired. His father sent him to school after school—Merchant Taylors, then Lostock, then Market Drayton. None held him long. He was intelligent, undeniably so, but possessed by a restless, uncontainable energy that refused to sit still for Latin or sums.

He was a force without purpose. And that, in 18th-century England, was a dangerous thing.

At home, his father grew cold. Robert was a disappointment, a wasted opportunity. He had failed at civility, at schooling, at decorum. A second son might have been groomed for the Church, or law. But Robert? He was now just a burden.

At seventeen, he was sent away.

Not to university. Not to military academy.

To India.

A clerkship with the East India Company in Madras was arranged—a humble position, bought with favors and family connections. It was a way to save face, to send the troubled boy far from England, far from scandal, and maybe—just maybe—make something useful of him.

When Robert Clive boarded the *Cadiz Merchant* in 1743, he did not weep for home. He looked back once at the gray cliffs of England, then turned his face east and did not look again.

He was nineteen.

The voyage took more than a year.

Disease stalked the decks. A dozen men died before rounding the Cape. Clive caught a fever near Mozambique and spent two weeks raving in his cot, imagining the devil pacing the length of the hold. He recovered, thinner but unchanged.

When they reached Madras in 1744, it was not the India he had imagined.

There was no gold in the streets, no marble palaces open to the ambitious. There was heat—choking, endless heat. There was dust. There was language he did not understand and customs he found maddening. And there was the Company—slow, bureaucratic, and dull.

He was assigned to the accounting house. A clerk's life.

Nine hours a day, hunched over ledgers, transcribing inventories of pepper and indigo, logging shipments, calculating tariffs, documenting the taxes of Indian rulers he would never meet.

He lived in a cramped apartment above a warehouse, with rats for company and the smell of spice bleeding into his skin.

At night, he read. Not trade manuals or Company histories—but *Plutarch. Caesar. Xenophon.* Stories of men who had shaped empires, not measured them.

He hated Madras. He hated the men who governed it. And he hated himself for being one of them.

By 1746, he'd had enough.

He borrowed a pair of dueling pistols from a fellow clerk—ostensibly for target practice. He took them to the edge of the city, where the jungle began, thick and indifferent.

He loaded one.

He placed it against his temple.

And pulled the trigger.

Click.

Nothing.

He tried again with the second.

Click.

Again, nothing.

He sat down in the grass, hands shaking, drenched in sweat. Then, slowly, he began to laugh.

It wasn't relief. It was rage.

The world wouldn't even let him die properly.

When he returned to the city, he was different.

Quieter, yes—but with something behind the eyes. Something sharp. Purposeful.

The fire that had once been wild was now directed. Focused.

He returned the pistols and thanked the man who had lent them.

Then he requested a transfer to the Company's militia.

The East India Company's militia was not, strictly speaking, a professional army. It was an awkward patchwork of adventurers, native sepoys, half-trained European volunteers, and a few retired officers clinging to the last embers of empire. Its ranks were held together by gold, promises, and the mutual hatred of the French.

Clive fit in immediately.

His first assignment was simple: assist in the defense of Madras. The war between Britain and France—what they called the War of the Austrian Succession back in Europe—had reached Indian shores, and with it came blood, confusion, and opportunity.

In 1746, the French seized Madras. The Company garrison folded in days. Clive and a small group of English officers fled the city under cover of night, disguised as sepoys, slipping through enemy lines with muskets wrapped in cloth and hearts pounding with shame and fury.

They retreated to Fort St. David, south of Pondicherry. There, Clive's military career began in earnest—not because he was trained, but because he was brave.

Recklessly brave.

He volunteered for every patrol, every raid, every half-suicidal scouting mission through enemy-held jungle. He was wounded twice—once in the shoulder by a French bayonet, once in the thigh by an arrow fired by an ally who mistook him for the enemy.

It didn't matter.

Clive discovered in war what he had never found in school or society: clarity.

He understood fear. He mastered logistics. He memorized terrain, learned local languages, studied French tactics, and absorbed native politics faster than most senior officers.

And most of all—he hated losing.

In 1748, during the Siege of Pondicherry, Clive served under Major Stringer Lawrence, one of the few professional soldiers the Company had in India. Lawrence noticed him at once.

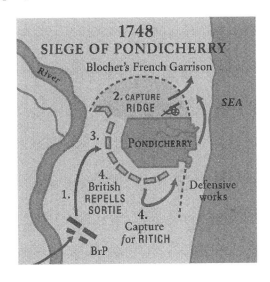

"Who's the mad bastard charging with half a dozen men into a fortified trench?" he asked.

"That's Clive," an aide replied.

Lawrence summoned him after the battle.

"You should've been dead."

Clive shrugged. "The French weren't aiming very well."

"You want to be an officer?"

"Yes," Clive replied, instantly.

Major Stringer Lawrence

He got the commission.

It was the beginning of his rise—and the beginning of something else. The transformation of the Company itself.

Because the East India Company was no longer just a trading enterprise. It was becoming a state. And men like Clive were the reason.

By 1751, war had spread across the south of India. The British and French weren't just fighting each other anymore—they were backing rival Indian princes, turning regional disputes into proxy wars. The Carnatic, once a Mughal province, had become the chessboard of empire.

A vast coastal region in southeastern India, Carnatic had fallen into civil war after the death of its nawab. Two claimants emerged: Chanda Sahib, supported by the French, and Mohammed Ali, backed by the British. As the two factions clashed across the plains of Tamil Nadu, Clive—then a junior officer—watched opportunity forming like storm clouds on the horizon.

In August of that year, Mohammed Ali, driven from his capital at Trichinopoly, begged the British at Madras for help. Most of the Company's troops were already committed elsewhere, and its governors hesitated. But Clive proposed something bold: strike at Arcot, the symbolic capital of the Carnatic. Not to hold it—just to take it. To shock. To unbalance.

Clive's moment had come.

Chanda Sahib, the French-backed candidate for Nawab of the Carnatic, had seized power and was moving to crush British influence in the region. Clive proposed something radical: a strike at Arcot, the symbolic heart of the province. If they took the city, it would undermine Chanda Sahib's legitimacy and rally native support to the British cause.

His superiors scoffed.

Arcot was heavily garrisoned. Clive had no formal command experience. The operation was suicidal.

He insisted.

They gave him 210 sepoys, 120 European soldiers, and three small cannons.

It was enough.

Clive led his ragtag force through monsoon storms and hostile jungle to the gates of Arcot. The city's defenders—caught off guard by the sheer audacity of the attack—fled after a brief bombardment.

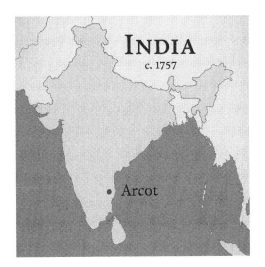

But that was only the beginning.

Within days, Chanda Sahib's son, Raza Sahib, returned with a force ten times the size of Clive's. He laid siege to the city, confident it would fall within the week.

It lasted fifty days.

Clive turned Arcot into a fortress. He inspired his men with discipline, humor, and an almost religious defiance. He refused to eat more than his troops. He personally manned the guns.

When a shell struck the roof of his command post, he brushed dust from his coat and continued issuing orders.

When Raza Sahib offered terms, Clive replied by shelling his camp.

On the fiftieth day, the siege broke. Reinforcements arrived from Madras. Raza Sahib retreated. Arcot was saved.
England took notice.

Parliament debated the "Clive of India." The press sang his praises. Company shares soared. And in the bazaars of India, his name became legend.

But Clive wasn't finished.

He had tasted command. And he wanted more.

When his term expired in 1753, he returned to England—not as a disgraced clerk, but as a war hero.

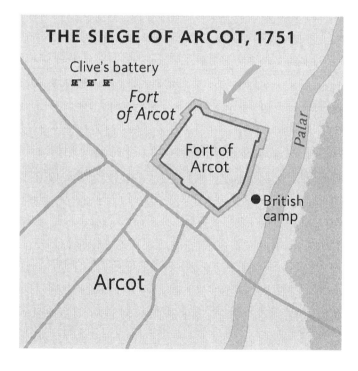

THE SIEGE OF ARCOT, 1751

Clive's battery

Fort of Arcot

Fort of Arcot

Palar

British camp

Arcot

Chapter 2: The Return and Rejection

The dockhands at Portsmouth hardly noticed the man stepping off the gangplank.

Dressed modestly, a worn coat pulled tight against the gray English drizzle, Robert Clive could have passed for any mid-level Company man returning from the East. He didn't look like a war hero, let alone the architect of one of Britain's most audacious military victories.

But inside the weather-beaten trunk that followed him down the ramp was a fortune.

Clive returned to England in 1753 with over £30,000 in private wealth—more than a lifetime of salaries for most Company officials. He had collected it in war bonds, captured goods, land grants, and subtle gifts from grateful allies. Every rupee had been earned in blood.

And yet, London was unimpressed.

The East India Company board, while officially grateful, offered no honors. Parliament made no mention of his victories.

He was not invited to court. No statues, no processions, no parade of triumph awaited him. In England, Clive was not a hero. He was a curiosity. An upstart. A merchant soldier who had become dangerous.

The aristocracy turned their noses up at the idea of a man gaining fame without pedigree. Clive's reputation, forged in the heat of Arcot, meant little to the powdered men who had never seen India and never intended to.

He was given a pension—modest—and expected to vanish into landed obscurity.

Instead, he bought a country estate.

Claremont House in Surrey became his new war room. From there, Clive began to rebuild his future. He studied politics. Courted allies. Married well—Margaret Maskelyne, the daughter of a respectable family with a brother who would soon become Astronomer Royal. She was cultured, composed, and precisely the sort of woman who could raise his social standing.

They honeymooned in Bath, where whispers followed them in drawing rooms and teahouses.

"He's made of Company gold," some muttered.

"A butcher," said others, "dressed like a gentleman."

Clive heard them. And remembered.

He never stayed long in any one place. He traveled to London, then to Ireland to visit his family, then back to Claremont. He tried writing a memoir but tore up the manuscript halfway through the first chapter.

He tried hunting, but the fox offered no satisfaction.

He tried Parliament.

In 1754, Clive was elected as Member of Parliament for St. Michael, a Cornish borough small enough to be bought outright.

He took his seat in Westminster, surrounded by men who neither respected nor trusted him. He spoke little. Voted as expected. Endured the slow torture of British politics with quiet disdain.

One evening, during a dinner with a group of Company directors, he was asked why he had returned to England at all. Clive paused, sipped his wine, and replied, "I came to see if it was worth saving."

He wasn't invited again.

By 1755, he had had enough.

The Company came calling once more. Bengal was in turmoil. French influence was growing. Calcutta's position was weakening. And the new Nawab—Siraj ud-Daulah—was rumored to be unstable, hostile to British interests.

And then the Black Hole incident happened.

Holwell published his harrowing account fueling British outrage and support for retaliation.

The press.

The people.

Parliament.

Even the Royals.

Everyone was asking for justice. And no one wanted to wait.

The Company was in a bind. They needed to restore order and their reputation. And they needed someone to do it fast and efficiently.

It was not a complicated choice.

They offered Clive a new commission: Governor of Fort St. David, with command of military operations in Bengal if conflict arose.

It was a demotion in title. But Clive saw the truth.

This wasn't a job. It was a second chance.

He accepted immediately.

Before departing, he visited Claremont one last time. Walked its gardens. Touched the stone columns of the house he had bought with blood money.

He kissed Margaret goodbye.

Then he boarded ship.

This time, he did not look back.

The voyage to India was faster the second time, though no less punishing.

Clive had been at sea before. He knew the routines, the dangers, the oppressive boredom. He passed the time reviewing dispatches from the Madras Council, rereading Holwell's latest reports from Bengal, and sketching theoretical battle plans in the margins of Company correspondence.

But this time he was not just a young officer returning to a war zone. He was a man with enemies in every direction—French traders, rival nawabs, cautious Company bureaucrats, and perhaps most dangerous of all, his own reputation.

He arrived in Madras in early 1756 to the sound of distant thunder and the heavy scent of wet earth. The monsoons had not yet broken, but they were coming.

At Fort St. David, he found things as he expected: under-defended, underfunded, and overseen by men far more interested in managing ledgers than managing threats.

Clive changed that quickly.

Within a week, he'd doubled training drills, reprimanded officers for sloppy discipline, and demanded fresh reports from every outpost between the coast and the interior. He pressed local merchants for intelligence and sent Company agents north to probe the situation in Bengal. Rumors trickled back slowly, carried on caravans and riverboats: Siraj ud-Daulah had grown paranoid, hostile. He was reorganizing the military. He had ordered arrests of English agents. He had threatened to expel the Company entirely from Calcutta.

Clive asked for permission to intervene preemptively.

The Madras Council hesitated.

They worried about overreach. About provoking the French. About the cost. They preferred a strategy of containment, negotiation.

Clive exploded in a rare display of temper. "Containment is not strategy," he said. "It's surrender with better diction."

He argued that waiting would only embolden Siraj. That the Company's position in Bengal was untenable without a show of force. That the massacre in the Black Hole—though yet un confirmed—could not go unanswered.

Eventually, the Council relented.

Clive was granted provisional command of a mixed force— Royal and Company troops—and given liberty to act as he saw fit "in the defense of Company holdings and honor."

That was all he needed.

He moved quickly, assembling a joint expedition with Admiral Charles Watson of the Royal Navy. The plan was straightfor- ward: sail north along the Bay of Bengal, rendezvous with any loyal forces near Falta, and retake Calcutta.

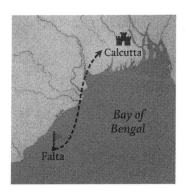

But in war, nothing is straightforward.

The expedition faced delays before it even set sail. Powder shipments were late. Rations spoiled. Several sepoy companies mutinied after being denied pay. Clive had two men publicly flogged and promised gold to the rest.

By November 1756, they were finally at sea.

The voyage north was treacherous. Monsoon swells battered the transport ships. One vessel sank in open water, taking thirty men and two cannons with it. Clive spent most of the voyage sleepless, walking the decks in silence, watching the horizon like a hawk.

When they reached the Hooghly, the real work began.

The terrain was a nightmare—dense jungle, flooded roads, and narrow canals infested with leeches and disease. Clive led the advance personally, driving his officers harder than they'd ever known. He rationed powder, reorganized supply lines, and sent scouting parties upriver to map enemy positions.

He made it clear: Calcutta was not to be taken. It was to be *reclaimed.*

As they approached the outskirts, Clive paused his men on a rise overlooking the city. Fort William stood in the distance, blackened and silent.

He turned to Admiral Watson and said, "When we are finished here, they will never forget the name."

They struck the next morning.

British cannon fire roared from the ships on the river. Clive's infantry advanced through smoke and mud, using the old ditches for cover. The Nawab's garrison—underpaid, under-manned, and disorganized—fell apart within hours.

When Clive entered the fort, he found what he had expected: ruin, rot, and a single dungeon cell that history would not forget.

He ordered it opened.

The guards hesitated.

"Do it," Clive commanded.

The door creaked open.
The chamber was dark, cool, and empty.

But in the silence, Clive could still hear them.

Screams. Gasps. Scraping nails on stone.

Holwell's ghost. And the ghosts of the nameless dead.

Clive stood there for a long time.

Then he stepped outside and summoned his officers.

"This," he said, "is why we will do this."

As they outfitted ships in Madras harbor, Clive moved among the crews like a man possessed. He inspected every musket. Reviewed every map. Met with merchants to arrange emergency supplies. He sent scouts to locate friendly zamindars along the river. He wrote letters to old allies in the Bengal courts.

He knew this campaign would be different. Not a skirmish over tariffs. Not a proxy war with the French.

This was a chance to break Bengal wide open.

To make it British.

Before sailing, he paid a final visit to Margaret.

Their reunion had been brief. She had come to India against her better judgment—sick often, anxious in the heat, disinterested in politics. But she loved him, and Clive, in his way, loved her.

"Must you go?" she asked quietly as he packed his trunk.

"Yes."

"There are others. Let someone else—"

"There's no one else."

She said nothing more.

At dawn, he boarded the *Tyger* and watched the coast fall away. The voyage north was slow and tense. Monsoon winds pushed back against their progress. A merchant sloop capsized off Vizagapatam. One of the sepoys fell overboard and was never recovered.

Clive did not sleep well. He sat often at the prow, sketching battle lines into the margins of his journal. He had fought before. He had killed. But this was different. This was history.

At Falta, near the mouth of the Hooghly River, the fleet regrouped. The banks were high with floodwater. The jungle teemed with snakes and fever. But ahead—just fifty miles upriver—lay Calcutta.

Clive looked inland and felt it in his bones.

Everything was about to change.

The march to Calcutta was a trial by water, mud, and disease.

From Falta to Fort William, every step was contested not by enemy forces, but by the land itself. The Hooghly River swelled its banks daily, swallowing roads and collapsing footpaths. Jungles choked with vines and leeches crept toward the Company column. And the heat—thick, wet, suffocating—pressed down like the hand of some unseen god, daring the British to push forward.

Clive's column was a mosaic of contrasts. Crisp-coated English officers walked beside barefoot sepoys. Bullocks pulled cannon carriages through sludge while Brahmin guides read signs in the trees. The Royal Navy's longboats escorted the column from the water, occasionally shelling the riverbanks to drive off opportunistic raiders.

At night, they camped in marshy clearings. Men fell sick from dysentery and fever. One lieutenant went mad under the sun and tried to shoot the moon. He was restrained and put on a transport back to Madras.

Clive remained unshaken.

He rode near the front, never far from the advance scouts, and never far from his artillerymen. He checked ammunition twice daily, interrogated couriers for news from the north, and memorized the geography of every bend in the river. He knew that this campaign would define him—not just in India, but in London.

And every mile gained brought him closer to the scene of the crime: the dungeon at Fort William.

The memory of Holwell's letter was burned into him. He could see it every time he closed his eyes: a black cell, bodies stacked like timber, air thick with death. A punishment not for soldiers, but for insects.

He would not let it go unanswered.

On the seventh day, they encountered the first true resistance.

A Bengali outpost—lightly fortified, garrisoned by around a hundred men—attempted to block a crucial crossing. Clive ordered a flanking maneuver, and his sepoys outmaneuvered the defenders in under an hour. Twenty enemy troops were killed, and the rest fled into the forest.

Clive paused to interrogate the local commander, who had been captured alive.

"Where is the Nawab's army?" he asked through an interpreter.

"Scattered. Some in Calcutta. Some marching. But they do not expect you so soon."

Clive nodded.

"Good."

The prisoner was released unharmed—an act of calculated mercy. Clive wanted news of his arrival to spread.

By the tenth day, they reached the outer edges of Calcutta.

The city—once the Company's crown jewel in Bengal—had become a symbol of humiliation. Burned homes. Looted shops. Native civilians wary of both the Nawab's soldiers and the English newcomers. But Fort William still stood, battered but recognizable.

Clive surveyed the defenses from a rise. His officers gathered around, eager.

"Is it strong?" one asked.

Clive grunted. "Strong enough for fools. But not for Bengal."

That night, he issued his final orders.

At dawn, the assault began.

It started with naval bombardment. Admiral Watson's ships opened fire on the fort's river-facing wall, shaking the very foundation of the old structure. Clive's artillery joined from the land, pounding the eastern wall where Siraj's men had made camp.

The response was disorganized. Siraj's troops, poorly trained and poorly paid, returned fire with musket volleys that fell short. After four hours, Clive sent in his sepoys to press the breach.

The defenders crumbled.

By mid-afternoon, the Union Jack flew once more over Fort William.

Clive entered through the main gate on foot, boots caked in mud, flanked by his officers. Inside, the smell of death still lingered beneath the fresh plaster and lime.

He ordered a full inspection of the fort.

He walked through the offices, the barracks, the powder magazines—and at last, the dungeon.

It had been scrubbed. The walls repainted. The vent cleared.

But he saw it.

Not the cell, but the memory.

He stood in the center of the room and let the silence sink in.

Then he turned to Holwell, now recovered and reinstated.

"We rebuild," Clive said quietly. "And then we march."

"March where, sir?"

"To Murshidabad."

He stepped out into the sun.

"And we do not stop."

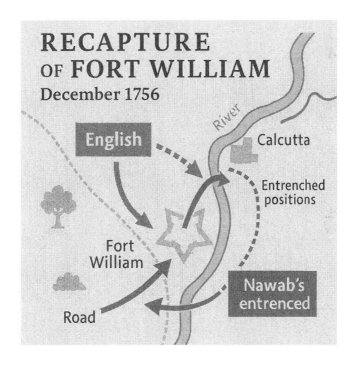

Chapter 3: Baptism by Fire

It began, as it so often did, with a letter.

Even before the smoke had cleared from the retaken walls of Fort William, dispatches flew in every direction. Messages to Madras, to London, to the Dutch at Chinsurah, and most importantly—to Murshidabad, capital of Bengal.

Siraj ud-Daulah had not expected the British to recover so quickly. He had assumed their retreat at Calcutta was final, their spirit broken, their governor disgraced. But Clive's counterattack changed everything. It was not just a retaking of a fort—it was a declaration of war.

Siraj was enraged. And rattled.

He issued orders for his army to march south. All Company activities in Bengal were to be halted. Englishmen found in Nawab-controlled territories were to be arrested or killed. His generals—many of whom quietly doubted his judgment—scrambled to organize the vast, bloated forces of the Nawab's army.

But Clive had already moved.

Even as reinforcements trickled into Calcutta, he was already pressing outward—fortifying British control over nearby towns and villages. He captured the riverside outpost of Budge Budge in a lightning raid, then marched inland toward the town of Hooghly, securing a key river crossing.

In late January 1757, Siraj's army—over 40,000 strong—descended from the north. Clive had fewer than 3,000 men.

The Nawab's troops halted at the outskirts of Calcutta. Siraj sent an envoy, demanding that the British leave Bengal at once, abandon Fort William, and pay restitution.

Clive replied with cannon fire.

The ensuing battle was chaotic and short. Siraj's forces attempted to storm the east wall of the fort but were met with a barrage of grapeshot and musket fire. Sepoys under Clive's command launched a flanking maneuver through a nearby canal path, catching the enemy off guard. The Nawab's troops broke ranks and retreated in disorder.

It was the first time Siraj tasted direct defeat.

Clive did not pursue. He didn't need to.

The message had been sent.

What followed was a strange and tense stalemate. Siraj withdrew to camp further upriver and sent word he was open to negotiations. Clive, recognizing the opportunity, agreed. The two sides exchanged letters over several days, during which

Clive played a delicate game—pretending interest in peace while secretly stoking rebellion inside the Nawab's own court.

He met in secret with emissaries of Mir Jafar, the discontented commander of Siraj's army, and Jagat Seth, the influential banker with the means to fund a coup. Clive offered everything the Company could promise: wealth, security, recognition, and power. In return, all he wanted was Siraj's removal—and a Nawab who would bow to British trade interests.

The plan took shape quickly.

Mir Jafar would march with Siraj's army as planned, but at the decisive moment—on the battlefield—he would withdraw his support. The betrayal would fracture the Nawab's command and leave him vulnerable. Once Siraj was defeated, Clive would ensure Jafar's installation as Nawab.

But betrayal, as Clive knew, was a dangerous currency. It had to be earned. And bought.

The Company guaranteed payment. Clive signed a treaty— never intended for public eyes—recognizing Mir Jafar as the "rightful ruler of Bengal." Jagat Seth would disburse the necessary funds once Clive won the battle. Every signature sealed the fate of a kingdom.

Still, Clive was not content to wait.

He wanted a test. A moment to probe the Nawab's strength.

And so, he planned a raid.

The target: the Nawab's encampment north of Calcutta, where Siraj had left behind a contingent to guard a critical supply depot and watch the river approaches.

It was a night assault. Rain poured in sheets, muffling the sound of boots and blades.
Clive led the vanguard himself.

Through jungle paths and narrow causeways, the British column crept toward the outer edge of the enemy camp. They wore stripped-down gear, no armor, no coats—just powder, blades, and speed.

At Clive's signal, they struck.

Gunfire erupted from the trees. Sepoys poured into the outer tents, bayonets flashing in the torchlight. Panic spread like fire. The enemy, caught in sleep and disarray, stumbled over themselves trying to form ranks.

Clive pushed forward, sword drawn, barking orders in English and Hindustani. A sentry lunged at him with a curved blade; Clive parried, then struck the man down with the butt of his pistol.

The entire raid lasted less than twenty minutes.

When it was over, dozens of the Nawab's men lay dead or wounded. The rest had fled into the trees. The British captured powder, food, and two officers who were promptly interrogated.

It wasn't a major victory.

But it was a message.

Clive wasn't just a trader with guns. He was a predator.

And he was hunting.

In the days that followed the raid, the landscape of Bengal held its breath.

Siraj's army retreated north to a fortified position near the village of Plassey, nestled beside the Bhagirathi River. The camp sprawled for miles—tents, elephants, camel trains, powder carts, and banners flapping in the rising heat. It was a show of strength, but it was also a bluff. Behind the spectacle, Siraj's court had begun to unravel.

Inside his gilded tent, the Nawab paced like a man hunted.

His advisors gave conflicting reports. One day they assured him that the British had stalled. The next, they spoke of betrayal. That Mir Jafar had been seen meeting with Company agents. That Jagat Seth was moving silver out of Murshidabad under armed guard. That even his most loyal regiments were unsure who truly commanded Bengal now.

Siraj's rage boiled over.

He dismissed generals. He ordered arrests. He even threatened Mir Jafar directly during a war council, demanding an oath of loyalty under penalty of death.

Jafar gave the oath.

And then sent another messenger to Clive.

Clive, camped upriver with his forces, was already in motion.

He had grown impatient. The waiting game—the diplomatic exchange, the secret promises—had dragged on too long. War was coming. He could feel it in the air.

He called a council of war.

It was held beneath a canvas awning, away from the spies and the heat. His senior officers gathered: Eyre Coote, Kilpatrick, Major Grant, young officers with wary eyes and sun-darkened uniforms. There was tension. Not everyone supported the plan.

"Even if Mir Jafar betrays Siraj," one captain said, "we're still outnumbered nearly twenty to one."

Clive nodded.

"And if he doesn't?"

"Then we're dead."

He let the silence linger.

"I've seen worse odds," he said at last. "But not with this much at stake. If we win, we don't just break Siraj. We take Bengal."

He let that hang.

Not just a battle. A kingdom.

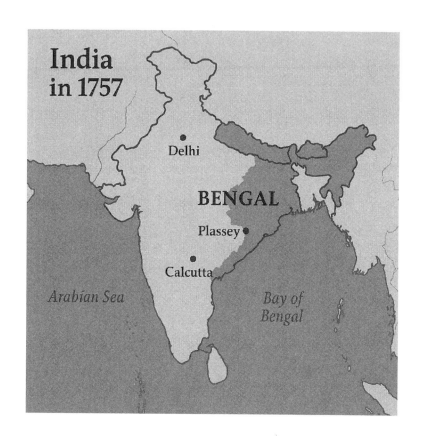

Chapter 4: Bengal in Turmoil

Bengal was the richest province in India.

A land of rivers and rice, of silk markets and spice bazaars, of palaces that shimmered in the sun and ships that lined the Hooghly from Calcutta to Murshidabad. Its population dwarfed that of most European nations. Its wealth fed the Mughal court. Its taxes propped up emperors. And now, its future balanced on the edge of Robert Clive's sword.

But Bengal was also a land fraying at the edges.

By the spring of 1757, Nawab Siraj ud-Daulah's rule was teetering. He had inherited a kingdom poisoned with intrigue—courtiers with private armies, bankers with more power than nobles, and generals who smiled in court while drafting their own succession plans. His youth, his temper, and his suspicion of the British only added fuel to the fire.

In the weeks following Clive's retaking of Calcutta, Siraj had withdrawn north to Murshidabad. Officially, he was regrouping. Unofficially, he was unraveling.

He summoned councils of war only to cancel them. He ordered purges of his advisors, accusing ministers of collusion with the British. Jagat Seth, the merchant prince who controlled the flow of Bengal's currency, was watched day and night by spies. Mir Jafar, the commander of his army, played the loyal servant—while writing letters to Clive in secret.
Siraj's paranoia became policy.

He raised taxes on Hindu landlords who he suspected of sympathizing with the Company. He arrested local rajas without trial. He punished entire villages for harboring British agents.

And yet, even as he cracked down, he could not escape the tightening noose of conspiracy around him.

In Calcutta, Clive had no illusions.

He knew Siraj was vulnerable—but not stupid. The Nawab still commanded the largest native army in eastern India. He still held the allegiance of key strongholds. And he still believed, despite the humiliation at Fort William, that he could negotiate from strength.

Clive began preparing for war.

Arcot had been a proving ground—Clive's first siege, where outnumbered Company forces held against chaos and heat to take the fort by sheer audacity. The men remembered.

But it was not just armies Clive now mustered—it was alliances.

continued to

He met with Jagat Seth personally. The banker came under heavy guard, escorted by camel and sedan from Murshidabad to Calcutta. Their conversation was short, polite, and electric.

"I can provide gold," Seth said. "But I cannot provide victory."

Clive nodded. "I'll bring the victory. You bring the throne."

From there, the plan moved quickly.

Jagat Seth reached out to Mir Jafar. Clive reached out to his own agents in the Nawab's court. They revived the idea of a replacement—someone from within Siraj's circle, someone with military credibility but enough ambition to break the chain of loyalty.

Mir Jafar was the perfect candidate.

He was old enough to command respect. Young enough to seize power. Popular with soldiers. Connected to the old guard.

And most importantly, desperate for the throne.
Clive promised him everything.

Company backing. Formal recognition. A signed treaty. A mountain of silver. And no interference in domestic affairs— just trade rights and the return of lost territory.

It was treason, plain and simple.

But it was efficient.

In March, Clive wrote to the Council at Madras:

"We have found a means of removing the Nawab with minimal bloodshed. A change of government may be effected with our involvement, to our benefit, and to the greater stability of Bengal."

Privately, he wrote to Watson:

"Jafar will betray. It is only a matter of time. All we must do is be present when he does."

Still, some of Clive's officers balked at the plan. They feared that relying on native factions could backfire. That Clive was building a house on sand.

But Clive dismissed them.

"Better to build a kingdom with turncoats," he said, "than to beg mercy from tyrants."

While the diplomacy unfolded behind closed doors, Clive turned to preparing his army.

He doubled infantry drills. He ordered fresh cannon carriages to be constructed from local teak. He instituted harsh discipline—any sepoy caught stealing, deserting, or sleeping on watch was flogged publicly.

He knew what was coming.

Siraj was not going to negotiate.

He was going to march.

The Nawab did not wait for diplomacy.

By early May 1757, Siraj ud-Daulah issued orders for his full army to assemble at Murshidabad. Over 50,000 men were summoned—infantry, cavalry, gunners, and support columns drawn from all corners of Bengal. The march southward began under blazing skies and the distant rumble of monsoon thunder.

His goal was simple: expel the British permanently. Crush them before they could conspire further. Retake Calcutta. Reassert control.

But even as the drums of war echoed through the countryside, betrayal stalked every campfire.

Mir Jafar's division, nearly one-third of the army, marched as ordered—but moved slowly, deliberately, and with eyes always cast behind. His officers followed him out of discipline, not devotion. Among his staff were two men already in contact with Company agents.

Jagat Seth's influence crept like a shadow across the battlefield.

Pay chests meant for loyal regiments arrived light or late. Rations were spoiled. Rumors flew that Siraj intended to arrest generals after the battle. Morale withered.

And still, the army marched.

At the same time, Clive made his final moves.

From Fort William, he began coordinating the advance with Admiral Watson. The Company fleet would secure the Hooghly River and provide fire support. Clive's land forces would strike from the mango groves near Plassey—narrowing the battlefield to neutralize the Nawab's superior numbers.

But before committing, Clive hesitated.

Not from fear—but from calculation.

He called a council of war on June 21, just two days before the planned confrontation. His officers gathered in a tent lit by oil lanterns and thick with tension. Maps lay unfurled across the table. Supply reports sat in neat stacks beside mugs of black tea.

"What if Jafar turns?" Major Kilpatrick asked. "What if it's all a ruse?"

Clive looked him in the eye.

"Then we fight anyway."

The room fell silent.

He leaned forward, tapping the map. "He has more men. More cannon. More elephants. But he has no will. No loyalty. No clarity. That is our advantage."

Still, uncertainty lingered. The Council remained divided. Clive dismissed them and sat alone in the dark. For hours.

Then, just before dawn, he made his decision.

The army would march to Plassey.

It was the defining moment of his career—and perhaps his life. The next day, he wrote a letter to the Madras Council:

"We proceed to meet the Nawab in the field. If our friends fulfill their promise, victory is certain. If not, we shall do our best to make it so."

Clive then issued his final orders.

The men were to move light—just essential rations, powder, and ball. The cannons would be positioned behind the mango grove. Scouts were to report any movement from Jafar's camp.

They left on June 22 at first light, a column of redcoats and sepoys winding their way through the jungle paths, muskets gleaming, faces grim. Rain threatened but did not fall. The sky held its breath.

It was a humid June morning. Steam rose from the jungle, thick and metallic. Clive's force—3,000 men, including around 900 European infantry, 2,100 sepoys, eight cannons, and a handful of engineers—traveled with discipline and precision. They cut through swampy paths, their boots sinking into the drenched soil of the Ganges delta.

By the evening of June 22, they reached a grove of mango trees near the village of Palashi—Plassey, to the British tongue.

It was here Clive would make his stand.

The grove offered cover. High ground. Natural barriers. It was a gift of terrain—and he seized it.

That night, scouts confirmed Siraj's army was encamped just beyond the rise—between 45,000 and 50,000 troops, including cavalry, artillery, war elephants, and Mir Jafar's own division.

Clive did not sleep.

He walked the lines. Spoke quietly with sentries. Checked the artillery placements by lantern light.

He paused by a grove of trees near the edge of camp and looked toward the enemy fires flickering on the horizon.

He could see it—just barely—Siraj's command tent, glowing like a jewel.

Chapter 5: The Enemy Assembles

The dust arrived before the men.

A brown cloud rose in the distance as Siraj ud-Daulah's army crept toward the fields of Plassey. From Clive's position beneath the mango trees, the haze looked like a wildfire crawling across the plain. It was morning, June 22, 1757. The skies were dry. The ground, still soft from the previous week's rain, steamed beneath the rising sun.

Clive watched it all through a spyglass, unmoving.

He had seen armies before—at Arcot, at Arni, at Kaveripak. But this one was different. It wasn't just the size. It was the silence that clung to it. The awkwardness of motion. The lack of confidence.

They were arriving because they were told to, not because they were ready.

He handed the glass to Eyre Coote without speaking.

Behind them, sepoys busied themselves with quiet preparation—repairing their powder horns, cleaning bayonets, checking shot. The British infantry lay in tight rows along the edge of the grove. Their boots were off, their uniforms open at the collar. They were resting, but it was a rest practiced in battle, timed to the hour, nerves on edge.

"Looks like half of Bengal's moving," Coote muttered, peering through the lens. "What do you think—forty thousand?"

Clive didn't answer. He was watching something else: a cluster of bright flags on the left side of the enemy's advance. Gold-trimmed, with green and red sashes. It was Mir Jafar's division.

It hadn't moved an inch.

"They're not in formation," Clive said. "See how wide the artillery line is? They've stretched it too far. Madan's in the center, not Jafar. They're not planning a full front."

Coote lowered the spyglass and looked at him. "Then what are they planning?"

Clive didn't blink. "They're waiting."

Waiting for what?

For orders?
For betrayal?

For God?

Siraj ud-Daulah's main camp began to unfold just outside of cannon range. Rows of tents went up hastily, marked by colored pennants indicating rank—blue for artillery command, yellow for cavalry, and the Nawab's own crimson standard with a golden sun stitched at its center. It flapped in the breeze like a challenge.

By midday, the Nawab's full force had arrived.

Over 50,000 men, if the estimates were accurate. Nearly 200 cannons—most cast in French or Persian forges. Cavalry numbering in the thousands, though lightly armed. And elephants—at least sixty—some armored, some bearing howdahs with musket platforms and small swivel guns.

It was a show of strength.

And, to Clive's practiced eye, an illusion.

Siraj's court had long prized spectacle over structure. His army reflected that. The ranks were disorganized. Most of the infantry were irregulars with no formal training, just conscripts pulled from landholdings or villages under the threat of taxation. Their uniforms varied. Their weapons were mismatched.

Their officers were noblemen, not soldiers.

But the danger wasn't in their disarray.

It was in their unpredictability.

A mob of fifty thousand, poorly led, could still overwhelm a disciplined army if it broke in the right place.

Clive knew this.

He turned away from the field and walked back toward the inner grove.

"Have the cannons dug in by nightfall. I want all eight ready by dawn."

Coote nodded and hurried off. Clive ducked beneath the canvas of the command tent, where Kilpatrick and two engineers were marking ranges on a large parchment map. The grove's natural rise gave the Company a slight elevation advantage, but only if the enemy came forward.

"We'll use the trees as cover," Clive said. "No open field shooting unless absolutely necessary. Have the sepoys stay low. I want them hidden until I give the signal."

Kilpatrick frowned. "And if they press from the left?"

"They won't," Clive said. "Not unless Jafar moves. And he won't."

A silence fell over the tent.

No one said what they were thinking: that if Clive was wrong, they would be wiped out by midday.

Just then, a scout entered the tent—a young Indian runner, breathless and muddy.

"The Nawab," he said, panting. "He holds war council tonight. In his pavilion. All commanders present."

Clive's eyes narrowed.

"Jafar?"

The scout nodded. "He sits beside him."

"Good," Clive said, and then, with a thin smile, "Let's see how close they sit by morning."

He dismissed the scout and stepped outside. The afternoon sun was lowering, casting long shadows across the field. He

looked again at the Nawab's sprawling camp—tents, banners, fires beginning to spark. So much motion. So much noise.
It was the noise of a machine that didn't know its own weakness.

Behind him, the grove rustled with quiet efficiency.

The British were ready. Eight field guns dug into earthen berms. Infantry sharpened bayonets. Sepoys cleaned their muskets with almost reverent care. Ammunition was stacked, rations portioned, water skins filled.

They did not sing.

They did not cheer.

They waited.

Clive stood at the edge of the grove and whispered to no one: "Let them come."

As night fell over the plains of Plassey, two camps stirred with equal restlessness.

In the Nawab's pavilion, the scent of rosewater masked the tension. Incense curled through the lattice windows, softening the air. Siraj ud-Daulah sat at the center of a circle of generals and ministers, flanked by guards who watched the room more closely than the fields beyond. The Nawab looked regal, but not composed—his hands clutched the arms of his chair too tightly, and his voice cracked when he spoke.

"Why haven't they attacked?" he demanded.

"They wait for our movement, Highness," said Mir Madan, his loyal artillery commander. "Their numbers are few. They cannot afford to provoke us."

"They cannot afford to breathe," muttered another officer, "unless Jafar gives them permission."

The room tensed.

Mir Jafar stood nearby, arms folded inside his robes, expression unreadable.

Siraj turned to him. "You've said little today."

Jafar bowed. "There is little to say until they move."

The Nawab's gaze sharpened. "Or until you do."

A heavy pause.

Jafar met his gaze calmly. "We serve you, Highness."

Siraj looked away, and the discussion moved on—battle formations, elephant charges, arc angles for cannon fire—but the weight of the room never lightened. Every man knew that loyalty was paper-thin. Every decision was wrapped in layers of second-guessing and self-preservation.

Outside the tent, campfires crackled as soldiers boiled rice, sharpened tulwars, whispered gossip, or played dice. The mood among the rank and file was wary but eager. Many had never seen combat. Most had never seen a British soldier. Their vision of war was ceremonial: a thunderous cavalry charge, followed by a scattering enemy. A clean victory. A celebration.

 Gold.

They didn't know what waited in the grove.

And the grove waited in silence.

Back among the mango trees, Clive sat cross-legged on a rolled blanket, studying the map under lamplight. He had removed his coat and unbuttoned his shirt. His skin glistened with sweat, but his breath was steady. Around him, the officers dozed in shifts—Kilpatrick, Coote, Grant—all within earshot, all within reach.

The grove was alive with quiet motion. Sepoys finished repairs on the breastworks. The cannons were cleaned, oiled, and aligned under the supervision of a wiry sergeant named Gibbons, who had trained under French artillerymen and now served with a ferocity usually reserved for men half his age.

Two scouts returned just after midnight. They crouched beside

Clive and reported in low voices.

"The Nawab's main force is encamped in three lines. Cannons in the front, elephants behind. No movement from Jafar."

"Camp secure?"

"Too secure. They're afraid."

Clive nodded.

"And the ground?"

"Soft near the river. The rest is dry. Good footing for infantry.

Poor for wheels."

Clive tapped the map with his finger. "They'll try to draw us into open ground. But they're not used to discipline. If they charge in disorder, we let them come. If they hold... we wait."

One of the scouts hesitated. "And if Jafar joins them?"

Clive stared at the map a moment longer.

"Then we lose."

He stood and walked to the forward line.

The mango grove narrowed into a natural bottleneck near its northern edge. There, the sepoys were posted behind woven screens reinforced with logs and earth. Bayonets glinted faintly in the moonlight. The grove itself had been turned into a fortress—traps laid, paths narrowed, trees marked for cover fire.

Clive crouched beside one of the sepoys and took his musket, inspecting it with quick efficiency.

"Name?"

"Ram Singh, sahib."

"First engagement?"

"Yes, sahib."

Clive handed the musket back.

"Stay low. Wait for my signal. And remember—discipline is worth a thousand men."

Ram Singh nodded, eyes wide.

Clive stood, brushing mango leaves from his coat, and returned to the rear.

He didn't sleep.

Instead, he wrote.

He took out a folded sheet of parchment, dipped his pen, and began a letter—not to Madras, not to the Company, but to Margaret.

My dearest,

If this is the last letter I write, know that I faced it all with clarity, not courage. I am outnumbered, perhaps outmaneuvered, but not outwitted. I know these men. I know how they think. I trust in my judgment more than I trust in luck.

He paused.

Scratched out the last line.

Then continued.

Tell the boys not to wear swords unless they mean to use them.

And tell them to always pay their debts—especially those owed in trust. I owe mine to a thousand brown-skinned men who march with me tomorrow because I asked them to. That is a debt I cannot repay.

He sealed the letter and gave it to his aide.

"If I fall," he said, "send it by ship. If I live, burn it."

By the first light of dawn, the fields were cloaked in a rising mist.

The Nawab's army stirred.

The elephants stamped and bellowed. Cannon crews began rolling their guns into position. War drums echoed faintly through the mist like the heartbeat of a sleeping beast.

In the grove, British soldiers rose in silence.

Clive took his place at the forward line, saber at his side, boots damp with dew.

He looked once more toward the horizon.

A few hundred yards of mud and mangoes stood between them.

Tomorrow, they would decide the future of India.

Then said quietly, "Let it begin."

Chapter 6: The Night Before

The moon was high and yellow when Robert Clive returned to his tent.

The ink had long dried on the secret promises—Jagat Seth's funding, Jafar's silence. But whether the pact would hold under fire… that was the gamble.

It was past midnight. The grove of mango trees had gone still, its branches heavy with dew. The only sounds were the occasional jingle of a sepoy's equipment and the low murmur of sentries trading whispers at the edge of the grove. Insects buzzed faintly in the humid air. No one was sleeping well.

Clive stood by his table for a long time, staring at the maps by lantern light. His tent was modest—bare canvas stretched taut over a timber frame, a single cot, a leather dispatch case, a writing table cluttered with reports and half-drunk tea. A flintlock pistol sat on the table beside his inkstand, casually placed but always within reach.

The latest intelligence confirmed what his instincts already told him.

The Nawab would not strike at dawn.

He had the numbers, the field, the momentum—but he lacked the will. That made him more dangerous. A hesitant enemy was harder to predict. He might retreat. He might delay. Or he might lash out blindly, forcing Clive to face the full weight of his fifty-thousand-man army before Mir Jafar's betrayal could unfold.

Clive rubbed his temple and stepped outside.

The night was dense and warm. A faint breeze stirred the leaves overhead. He made his way slowly toward the forward gun emplacements. The sepoys, awake but quiet, sat in clusters behind the breastworks. Some sharpened bayonets. Others sat with hands clasped, whispering prayers to Hanuman or Vishnu. A few simply stared into the dark, eyes unblinking, waiting for something to move.

Clive stopped beside a small group near the front.

"Sleep if you can," he said softly, in clear Hindustani.

A young sepoy looked up. "You do not sleep either, sahib."

"No," Clive said, "but I've done this before."

The men chuckled quietly.

He moved on.

By the time he returned to the command area, his officers were gathering—Coote, Kilpatrick, Major Grant, a few of the artillery captains, and a lieutenant from the engineers. They stood around the table as Clive rolled open the latest map.

"The Nawab will not attack first," Clive said. "But he will position himself to provoke. He'll try to draw us into the open. We don't oblige."

Coote folded his arms. "And if he advances on us directly?"

"Then we give ground slowly. Draw him into our guns. Once they're committed, we pivot on the left and break his flank." Kilpatrick pointed to the grove's edge. "Our cannon positions are solid, but we're light on reserves."

"We hold the center," Clive said. "Jafar will never engage until he's certain we have the upper hand. We give him that moment. And then we strike."

A silence fell over the group.

It was the kind of silence before a plunge—before the charge, before the breach, before the storm. Every man in the tent understood what waited outside. They were outnumbered nearly twenty to one. Their only advantage was precision—and treachery.

"Any word from Jagat Seth?" Coote asked.

Clive nodded. "Funds secured. Mir Jafar's men have been promised payment upon our victory."

"And if we lose?"

Clive didn't blink. "Then no one will be around to collect."

They dispersed after that, one by one, each man retreating to his own patch of earth, his own silence.

Clive sat alone in the tent.

He took up his journal—not the official Company ledger, but the small, leather-bound book he kept for himself. He opened it to a blank page, dipped his pen, and wrote:

June 22, 1757 – Plassey, Bengal

Tonight we sleep in the orchard. The enemy is camped in sight of our guns. I have seen armies in full strength, but this is not one. They are brittle beneath the surface. Their commanders do not speak as comrades. Their men have no belief. We do.
That is our weapon.

He paused, then added:

If this is my final entry, let it be known—I chose to strike, not to wait. Delay is death. Momentum is empire.

He closed the book.

Outside, thunder rumbled faintly in the distance. Not from clouds—but from hooves, cannon wheels, drums. The Nawab's army was preparing, too. Somewhere out there, fifty thousand men readied themselves to test the resolve of three thousand.

And somewhere among them, Mir Jafar lay awake, his thoughts caught between two futures.

One where he kept his word.

One where he didn't.

Across the field, the Nawab of Bengal did not sleep.

Siraj ud-Daulah paced the length of his tent with increasing agitation. The embroidered carpet beneath his feet was worn smooth from hours of restless circles. Candles guttered in the damp night air. Outside, his army lay blanketed in uneasy silence—elephants dozing in chains, cavalry units half-awake around dying fires, gunners trying to keep their powder dry beneath oilcloth.

Inside the pavilion, the war council had long since dissolved. Siraj had dismissed most of his generals in a fit of frustration after dusk. Only Mir Madan and a handful of personal guards remained.

"They do nothing," Siraj snapped for the fifth time. "They camp in a grove and mock us with stillness."

Madan, ever loyal, kept his tone calm. "It is their way. The English do not rush. They study. They wait."

"Then we shall give them something to study," Siraj growled. He stopped mid-stride and turned to a court scribe. "Draft an order. At first light, advance the center cannon line. Let them know we are not idle."

The scribe nodded quickly, ink already running from the humidity.

"And Jafar?" Siraj added, voice low. "Still no movement?"

"No, Highness," said Madan. "He keeps to his command post.

He offered no comment during today's review."
Siraj stared at the tent flap as if it might part to reveal a traitor.

"I should have removed him weeks ago."

Madan hesitated. "But you did not."

"No," Siraj whispered. "Because he is the only man whose betrayal I fear more than his loyalty."

The candlelight flickered. For a brief moment, the Nawab's face—so often concealed beneath jewels, ceremony, and command—was that of a boy. Tired. Cornered. Out of his depth.

He waved Madan away. "Go. Let me be."

Madan bowed and stepped out into the humid darkness, leaving Siraj alone with his thoughts.

Across the plain, in the mango grove, Clive still walked.

The British camp had quieted. The final patrols were making rounds. The guns were checked, double-checked, then covered with tarp. The sepoys lay curled on their bedrolls in their sweat-damp uniforms, rifles within reach.

Clive moved like a ghost among them.

Every few yards, he knelt. Not to pray, but to speak.

To a gunner: "Elevation looks right. Remember to wait for my signal."

To a sepoy: "You fire only when the man next to you fires. Not before. We do this as one."

To a sentry: "Eyes open. Listen to the elephants. They move before the cavalry does."

The soldiers responded with tired nods and the flat confidence of men who had seen this before—or trusted the man who had.

By the time he returned to his tent, the moon had passed over-head.

He lay down fully clothed, saber beside him, boots still laced.

And for a few hours, he slept.

Not deeply.

Not without dreams.

But enough.

Dawn broke with a hiss of mist off the Bhagirathi River.

In the Nawab's camp, elephants trumpeted as mahouts prod-ded them to standing. Cannon crews were already sweating, dragging their guns forward to new positions as per the night's orders. Cavalry commanders shouted across muddy paths. Si-raj's red banners flapped high in the windless morning air.

But something was wrong.

The cannons moved too slowly.

The officers took too long to assemble.

Jafar's division, still encamped on the left, remained utterly mo-tionless.

Siraj watched it all from his command post, teeth grinding be-hind his lips.

He barked orders for signal drums.

No reply.

He ordered a rider to Jafar.

The man did not return.

On the other side of the field, Clive was already in position.

He stood beside the central gun emplacement with Coote and Kilpatrick, his hand resting lightly on the hilt of his saber. The trees around them were full of dew. The mist had not yet lifted, but through the veil, they could see the movement—Siraj's guns repositioning, elephants shifting behind infantry lines.

"Do they know how to fight?" Kilpatrick asked, watching a cannon lurch forward and nearly tip.

"No," Clive said. "But they know how to die."

He turned to his adjutant. "Send word down the line. Positions hold until I say. Not a single shot until my mark."

The adjutant rode off.

To the left and right, British troops settled behind their screens.

They could hear the drums now—faint, irregular, uncertain.

In the center of the Nawab's army, Mir Madan urged his cannon crews forward, trying to inspire some coherence in the massed lines. His men responded, but hesitantly. The orders from above were unclear. Some thought the charge had been canceled. Others feared the English had trapped the grove.

The elephants refused to advance, unsettled by the rising smoke.

And all the while, Mir Jafar stood still.

His troops unmoving.

His eyes fixed not on the enemy—but on the Nawab's crimson standard in the center of the field.

Back in the grove, Clive looked toward the rising sun.

"It begins now," he said.

He raised his hand.

And all across the line, the barrels of eight cannons dropped slightly into final position.

Chapter 7: Opening Salvos

The first cannonball screamed through the grove just after sunrise.

It was not precise. It whistled high over the mango trees and landed in a patch of wet grass behind the British line, where it hissed and embedded itself harmlessly into the earth. A sepoy flinched. Another muttered a prayer. No one moved.

Then came the second.

Lower. Faster. It clipped a branch and sent leaves raining down like confetti.

Then came the third—and with it, the storm.

Siraj ud-Daulah's artillery opened fire in earnest. Dozens of cannons, some French-forged, others Mughal-cast, roared across the field, sending smoke rolling toward the grove. The ground shook. Birds scattered. Thunder cracked across the plain as round shot churned up dirt, splintered tree trunks, and sent debris cascading through the Company ranks.

Clive did not flinch.

He stood behind the first British cannon emplacement, hands clasped behind his back, eyes fixed on the enemy's central line. To his left, Captain Gibbons crouched over a six-pounder, barking orders to the gunnery crew in quick, practiced bursts.

"Range—two hundred! Hold! Fire!"

The cannon answered with a deep, guttural boom.
Its shot tore across the field and punched through a mass of Siraj's infantry. Screams followed. A riderless horse bolted back into the fog. More cannons spoke. Another volley.

The battle had begun.

And still, Clive waited.

Behind the grove's natural curtain of trees, the British line held firm. Muskets remained silent. Bayonets stayed down. Sepoys crouched in their firing lines, breathing steadily, eyes ahead. They could see the enemy now—vague shapes moving in the smoke, flashes of brass and red, the shimmer of sunlight on sword and scale.

The Nawab's army had not advanced yet. This was posturing. Pressure. A thunderous display of might meant to weaken resolve before the charge.

But Clive understood the language of battle.

And he could hear the hesitation behind the noise.

"They're probing," he said aloud to no one.

On the far left flank, near the river, the Nawab's cavalry began to spread. Lightly armored horsemen, hundreds strong, edged into the field. They did not charge. They circled.

Tested. Watched.

Clive followed their movement with sharp, birdlike attention.

"They're not sure where we are," he murmured.

And they weren't.

The grove concealed most of the British position. What looked like a tightly clustered orchard from the Nawab's side was in fact a layered defense: gunners up front, infantry behind cover, with sepoy marksmen hidden along interior paths.

Every tree had been accounted for. Every route measured.

The enemy was firing blind.
Still, the barrage continued.

A Company artilleryman screamed as a shot ripped through the parapet and struck his leg. A field surgeon dragged him to the rear. One of the cannons cracked its wheel on recoil and had to be replaced with the backup. Powder smoke clung to the grove like fog, turning the air acrid and hard to breathe.

Clive stepped forward.

"Return fire," he ordered.

Eight British guns answered as one.

The volley was precise, staggered, controlled. Each round shot aimed low, not at the bulk of the enemy, but at their cannon teams. The first few missed—bouncing in wet dirt, skipping past the Nawab's infantry. But then came the hits.

One cannon struck true, exploding against an enemy gun carriage in a burst of wood and fire.

Another ripped through a cluster of gunners mid-load.

The effect was immediate.

The Nawab's barrage began to stagger.

Back in Siraj's camp, the Nawab clutched the arms of his field throne as reports filtered in.
"Their guns are hidden!"

"We cannot reach them!"

"Our forward battery is broken!"

Siraj stood. "Then we advance! Order Mir Madan to bring the elephants forward!"

The command was relayed hastily—drums pounded, flags waved, riders galloped into the center. Across the field, Madan cursed as he heard the signal. He had not ordered this. His guns were not ready for a mobile advance. But the command came from the top—and it could not be disobeyed.

He ordered the first line forward.

Cavalry surged.

Infantry marched.

And behind them, elephants lumbered into the smoke.

In the grove, Clive watched the shapes emerge.

It was time.

"Stand by!" he called.

Muskets rose.

Bayonets gleamed.

Cannon crews reloaded in tight, flawless rhythm.

The enemy was coming.

Not a disciplined line—but a wave.

They came not as soldiers, but as thunder.

From the murky dawn mist, the Nawab's infantry surged forward—thousands of men in loose formation, some shouting, some silent, their turbans soaked with sweat and their muskets held high. The line was uneven, more a tide than a charge, with no fixed front, no coordinated march. Behind them, the elephants advanced with ponderous dread, trunks raised, riders shouting to guide them into position.

In the grove, Clive gave the signal.

"Fire!"

The front line erupted.

Muskets flashed in unison, a wall of smoke and heat that swallowed the trees and hurled lead into the advancing wave. The first ranks of Siraj's infantry buckled instantly—bodies collapsing into wet earth, men tripping over the fallen, chaos blooming with each volley.

Before the echoes had faded, the second Company volley rang out—this time from sepoys hidden behind tree trunks, firing in disciplined sequence. Their shots were low, aimed not for spectacle but to maim—knees, thighs, torsos.

Clive turned to his artillery crew. "Gibbons!"

The grizzled sergeant nodded. "Range: one-fifty!"

And still the elephants came.

Looming shapes of iron and bone, painted with war paint, howdahs rattling atop their backs, some with swivel cannons, others with musket platforms. A few lumbered directly toward the grove's center.

The British guns pivoted. Each crew loaded with chain shot— two iron balls linked by a length of chain, designed to tear through flesh and disrupt formation.

"Fire!"

The grove shook.

The chain shot screamed into the charging beasts.

One elephant took a blast to the foreleg and collapsed, scream- ing. Another, shot through the jaw, spun in confusion and turned—trampling its own men as it fled. Others slowed, eyes wide, trunks whipping madly.

The charge began to falter.

But the center pressed on.

Mir Madan's troops—better trained, better led—began to en- circle the British flank. Their cannons, now repositioned, be- gan pounding the grove from the side. One British emplacement was struck directly. Two gunners died instantly. A tree exploded into splinters above Clive's head.

"Left flank, hold!" Clive shouted.

Kilpatrick rushed to reinforce the line, leading a contingent of sepoys up the grove's slope. They dug in fast, exchanging fire with Madan's advancing musketeers. The air became a storm of powder and heat.

And all the while, Clive moved.

He was everywhere—checking cannon range, correcting formations, rallying troops with short, sharp commands. He passed a fallen sepoy, knelt briefly, and took the man's water flask to hand off to another soldier.

Above all, he watched for Jafar.

Across the field, the traitor's division stood still.

No movement. No sound. No support.

"Coward," Kilpatrick muttered as he returned to Clive's side, his arm bleeding from a graze.

"No," Clive replied. "Not yet."

He raised his glass again and studied the enemy line.
Madan's forces were the only organized unit still pressing.

The rest—cavalry, elephants, irregular infantry—were faltering. Some turned back. Some stood confused, their orders lost in the roar of cannon fire.

And then—finally—it happened.

A Company cannonball struck the center of the Nawab's personal guard.

A ripple ran through the field.

In the rear, Siraj's command platform shuddered. His flag dipped.

His voice cracked as he screamed: "Where is Jafar? Why does he not attack?"

There was no answer.

Back in the grove, Clive saw the flag falter.

He saw the enemy's momentum shift.

"They're breaking," he said.

Another volley.

Madan fell.

Clive didn't see the shot land, but the word spread fast. Siraj's bravest general, his most loyal commander, was gone. His body was dragged from the line, blood spilling across a rusted saber.

At that moment, the charge collapsed.

Not in an explosion, but in a gradual sag.

Men slowed. Some knelt. Others turned and ran.

Elephants wheeled around, smashing into their own lines.

The British advanced.

Not fast. Not reckless.
But deliberate.

Each step forward came with a new volley. Sepoys pushed out of the grove, using the trees as cover. British grenadiers followed behind, hurling explosives into pockets of resistance.

The enemy's cannon crews abandoned their posts.

Horses fled into the jungle.

Across the field, Mir Jafar remained still.

But his men no longer held their weapons. Some had begun walking away. Others dropped their swords. And as the Company flags emerged from the smoke, many simply turned and fled.

In the center of it all, Siraj ud-Daulah watched the end of his rule unfold.

He had no more orders.

Only disbelief.

He mounted a horse and rode—not to Jafar, not to the front, but to the rear.

He rode away from the smoke.

Away from the groves.

Away from his crown.

Chapter 8: The Center Holds

Before the field collapsed, before the victory was sealed, there had been a moment when everything nearly came undone.

It began with the cannons.

As the Nawab's right flank disintegrated and the elephants retreated in terror, a single cannon battery near the center of the enemy line held its ground. These were Mir Madan's most experienced gunners—men trained by French officers, hardened by campaigns along the Orissan coast. With their general dead and the center dissolving, they did not retreat. They fired.

Over and over.

At close range.

With frightening accuracy.

Their shot tore into the grove like thunderbolts. One Company cannon exploded, its crew scattered in pieces. A forward ammunition wagon caught fire and ignited a column of black smoke. The sudden explosion rocked the grove, momentarily blinding several regiments with heat and ash.

Clive, caught near the left-center, had to dive for cover.

He hit the ground behind a supply cart just as a round shot split the cart's wheel.

Kilpatrick rushed to his side, face bleeding from a shallow cut above his eye. "Sir! The center's cracking!"

Clive didn't rise.

He looked to the east, where two of the sepoy regiments were buckling under sustained fire.

They were pinned—flanked by musket volleys on one side and cannon bursts on the other. Their captains shouted over the din, trying to reform lines, but the smoke had thickened.

Visibility dropped to yards. Men began to break formation.

Just for a moment.

But a moment was all it took.

Clive rolled out from behind the cart and climbed onto its broken axle.

"Rally!" he shouted, voice cutting through the haze like a whip.

"Hold the line! Fix bayonets!"

His presence snapped the nearest officers back into motion.

One barked in Persian, another in Hindustani. Within seconds, the regiments were moving again—realigning under fire, stepping into the breach with grim determination. Clive grabbed a musket from a fallen soldier and pointed it toward the enemy battery.

"Gibbons!" he bellowed. "Give me two rounds on that cannon—now!"

Gibbons, crouched behind his remaining gun, nodded once.

He shouted for double powder.

The cannon fired.

The first shot missed—but the second struck true, cracking the enemy carriage and tossing one of the gunners backward like a rag doll.

That was the break.

Clive seized it.

He called for a charge—not a full advance, but a limited push to reclaim the center line.

Kilpatrick led the maneuver, taking sixty sepoys and thirty redcoats forward in a staggered sprint across the grove's open lane. They moved fast, under covering fire, and reached the ridge just as another enemy cannon misfired and jammed.

Close combat followed.

Bayonets met tulwars.

Muskets became clubs.

The Company men had discipline. The Nawab's troops had panic.

In five minutes, the center line was retaken.

By ten, the cannon battery had been silenced.

Clive reached the ridge and found Kilpatrick kneeling beside a wounded sepoy, wrapping a cloth around the man's leg with his own belt.

"We've got the ground," Kilpatrick said between breaths.

"But only just."

Clive nodded, looking over the carnage.

Dozens of bodies lay sprawled in unnatural poses.

Two mangled elephants lay still beside a shattered tree.

The center had held.

But barely.

He turned to the rear and called for reinforcements. Within minutes, fresh sepoy units were rotating into the line, relieving the wounded and dragging the dead behind the breastworks. Powder was redistributed. Officers checked firing angles.

Clive moved among them, pausing at each cluster of men.

"You stood your ground," he said.

"You earned this field."

He did not offer speeches.

Only presence.

And presence was enough.

The ridge at the grove's edge, once a natural feature barely noted on Clive's maps, had become the pivot point of the entire battle.

It was here that the storm of Plassey hit its hardest.
And it was here that the British line refused to break.
Even as the Nawab's cannons fell silent and Siraj's cavalry scattered into the rice fields, the center held—bloodied, scorched, but intact.

Clive stood now amid the scorched trees, watching as sepoy engineers reinforced the position. Logs were dragged into place to form an impromptu barricade. Wounded men were hauled to the rear on stretchers made from torn canvas and bamboo poles. A surgeon moved among them quickly, sleeves rolled, knife in hand, working without rest.

A junior officer approached, pale beneath his helmet. "Report from the eastern flank, sir. Minor resistance. Enemy disorganized. No countercharge."

Clive nodded.

"And the center?"

The officer glanced behind him, where the smoke still hung low. "Quiet. They've pulled back."

Clive turned slowly and surveyed the wreckage below.

It had not been a rout—but something worse: a war fought with half-hearted orders, muddled loyalties, and soldiers who died without knowing why. The enemy had not been defeated by strength. They had collapsed from within.

The real fighting, he knew, had been in this center grove.

Here, for twenty minutes that stretched like an hour, the battle could have gone either way.

If the sepoys had broken...

If the cannon had missed...

If Jafar had advanced...

But none of those things had happened.

And now the battlefield belonged to the Company.
At the base of the ridge, Kilpatrick leaned on a musket barrel, panting. His uniform was torn, one sleeve missing, his boots

thick with blood and dirt. "Damn fools almost had us," he muttered.

Clive walked down and stood beside him.

"They didn't," he said simply.

Behind them, the captured enemy cannon lay half-buried in mud. Clive placed one boot on its shattered axle and looked across the field. His eye caught movement in the distance— figures stumbling toward the north, away from the smoke, away from the banners.

"They're running," he said.

"Do we chase them?"

Clive shook his head. "No need. Let them carry the story."

He turned back toward the grove.

His men were regrouping. Redcoats washed powder from their hands in canteens. Sepoys passed around dried fruit and stale bread. No one cheered. There was no time for it. No energy. Just the stunned calm of survival.

Captain Gibbons arrived, limping slightly, one arm wrapped in a bandage. "Guns are still operable, sir. All but the second. She cracked when we doubled the charge."

Clive gave a slight nod. "She served."

Gibbons grinned through the grime. "She did."

News trickled in from all sides.

The Nawab's forces were dispersing. Entire regiments had melted into the countryside. Elephants were found tied to trees and abandoned. Cavalry units had dropped sabers and fled across the river. Even looters had been slow to arrive—too shocked by the scale of what had happened to take advantage of it.

And then, finally, the report Clive had been waiting for.

A rider from Coote's detachment arrived bearing a sealed message.

Clive cracked the wax with one gloved hand and read silently. Then he folded it once and tucked it inside his coat.

"Siraj is gone," he said aloud. "He's abandoned the field."

There was a long pause.

No reaction. Just breathing.

Coote himself arrived shortly after, his uniform soaked in sweat, face streaked with powder. He tossed his helmet to the ground and dropped onto a fallen log.

"God help me," he muttered. "I think we've done it."

Clive sat beside him.

He said nothing for a while.

The two men looked out over the field together—at the smoldering trees, the shattered cannons, the faint outlines of banners caught in the branches.

"This isn't a victory," Clive said finally. "It's a beginning."

Coote gave him a sideways glance. "I thought this was the end."

Clive shook his head.

"Not for us. And not for India."

He stood again, stretching his back, then looked toward the far end of the plain.

"Send word to Jafar," he said. "Tell him the road to Murshidabad is open."

Then, quieter:

"Tell him to be ready."

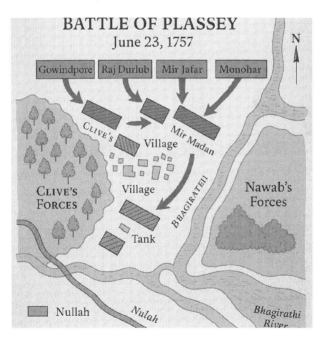

BATTLE OF PLASSEY
June 23, 1757
N

Gowindpore | Raj Durlub | Mir Jafar | Monohar

CLIVE'S
Village
Mir Madan
Village
CLIVE'S
FORCES
Nawab's
Forces
Tank

Nullah
Nulah
Bhagirathi
River

Chapter 9: The Storm Breaks

The rain came late.

Not from the sky, but from the soil—the black, loamy earth of the Hooghly plain kicked up into thick clods by boots, hooves, and blood. By midday, the mist had burned off, replaced by sun and powder smoke. The field stank of saltpeter, manure, sweat, and the iron tang of death.

But Clive was already moving.

His forces had broken from the mango grove and were now pressing into the disintegrating lines of the Nawab's army. Sepoys in disciplined ranks advanced through the haze, muskets at their shoulders, reloading in rotation. British grenadiers in red surged forward with bayonets fixed, their boots sinking into the wet grass, their eyes locked forward.

There was no cheer. No roar of triumph.

Just the rhythm of killing.

The Nawab's central cannon line had collapsed.

After Mir Madan fell—struck in the chest by British round shot while directing a final volley—there was no one left with the authority or the will to hold the forward line. His gunners abandoned their stations. Elephants, now panicked by the blasts and screams, fled back through the rear guard, trampling their own infantry.

What had begun as a charge now became a stampede.

But the storm had not yet finished breaking.

To the west, a pocket of resistance remained.

Three thousand of Siraj's musketeers, drawn from Afghan mercenaries and his personal bodyguard, regrouped near a small stand of banyan trees. They formed a ragged square and fired sporadically into the advancing Company line.

Clive saw the movement and dispatched Coote.

"Break them. Use the guns if needed. But quickly."

Coote saluted and peeled off with a detachment of sepoys and two six-pounders, wheeling them through the muck with grim determination. The grenadiers fanned wide, flanking the square and driving a wedge into its eastern corner.

The banyan grove became a killing floor.

After ten minutes, it was silent.

Across the broader field, the Company line advanced methodically—step, fire, reload, repeat. There were no wild rushes. No glory charges. Clive knew the enemy was disoriented but still dangerous. He would not risk overextension.

His men had orders: hold formation, conserve ammunition, press the advantage, but do not break ranks.

It worked.

With each step, more of Siraj's army folded. Cavalry commanders galloped aimlessly along the perimeter, unsure of where to commit. Couriers disappeared. Supplies burned. Officers who had boasted of swift victory now fled in disguise, casting off turbans and sashes to escape recognition.

The most telling sight came from the left flank.

Mir Jafar's division remained frozen.

Ten thousand men.

Fully armed.

Fully silent.

Clive had half-expected Jafar to turn his troops on Siraj's army in a final display of betrayal. But the man remained cautious.

Cowardly, even. He did nothing. And it was precisely that nothing that sealed the Nawab's fate.

Clive turned to Kilpatrick.

"Signal the left to extend."

Kilpatrick lifted his bugle and blew two sharp notes.

On cue, the sepoy regiments on the Company's left surged outward, curling around the Nawab's remaining line like a pincer.

No resistance met them. Many of Siraj's men dropped their weapons and fled. Others threw down their standards and knelt.

It was not a rout.

It was evaporation.

By early afternoon, the battlefield was a patchwork of corpses, broken weapons, shattered gun carriages, and abandoned gear. Smoke still hung low, but the firing had mostly stopped.

Clive stood beside a captured Nawabi cannon, its barrel cracked, its wheels torn off.

A young lieutenant approached, blood on his uniform.

"Sir, reports say the Nawab has fled the field."
Clive didn't smile.

"Where?"

"Toward Murshidabad. Alone. His guard deserted him."

Clive nodded. "Let him run."

The lieutenant hesitated. "Do we pursue?"

Clive looked out over the field.

He saw his men picking their way through the wreckage. He saw wounded sepoys helping one another to the rear lines. He saw Jafar's troops still standing motionless in the far distance, like statues watching the fall of an empire.

"No," he said. "Not yet."

He turned back to the grove, where his cannon crews were already cleaning their guns.

"We hold the field. That's enough."

And it was.
Plassey was his.

By late afternoon, the battlefield no longer belonged to the Nawab—or to anyone.

It was a wasteland of torn standards, abandoned weapons, and blood-soaked tunics half-buried in the churned soil. Clive stood at the ridge just beyond the grove, flanked by Coote and Kilpatrick, surveying the field through a spyglass smeared with powder soot.

The smoke had thinned. The heat had risen.

From their position, they could see the full arc of what had occurred: the broken center, the collapsed right, and the inert shadow of Mir Jafar's unmoved division like a smudge of ink on the battlefield's edge.

"They never fired a shot," Kilpatrick said, gesturing to Jafar's troops.

"They didn't have to," Clive replied.

He lowered the glass and turned to Coote. "Send word to Jafar. Tell him the time has come. The field is ours. The next move is his."

Coote hesitated. "Do we trust him?"

Clive looked back at the empty plains. "No. But we've given him no choice."

Word spread quickly through the British line: Siraj had fled, his army shattered. A thin cheer rose among the sepoys—a ripple of exhausted elation, more relief than triumph. British soldiers slumped to the ground where they stood. Water flasks were passed down the lines. Officers counted their dead in silence.

Clive said nothing.

He walked the battlefield instead.

He passed ruined gun carriages, their wheels splintered and burned. He stepped over the twisted bodies of infantry and cavalry alike—Nawabi troops in silk sashes and Company men in red tunics now soaked black. He paused at a fallen elephant, its eyes wide and unseeing, its tusks broken, a howdah cracked in half beside it.

Near the center of the field, he stopped at the place where Mir Madan had fallen.

His body had already been stripped of armor. The ground around him was torn and muddy, stained dark. A sepoy stood nearby, watching. Clive asked no questions. He simply nodded, then turned away.

Back at camp, the wounded were being treated in the shade of the grove. British surgeons moved swiftly, sleeves rolled, hands red. Sepoy medics wrapped bandages, boiled water, and whispered prayers over the most severe cases. For every man who had fought, there was another tending to those who could not stand.

Clive returned to his tent and removed his coat for the first time all day. It peeled off stiff with sweat and blood. He sat at his writing desk and opened the Company ledger.

He stared at the blank page for a long time.

Then he wrote:

June 23, 1757

The field is ours. The Nawab has fled. The guns are silent. Mir Jafar has yet to declare himself, but the outcome is no longer in question. We are outnumbered, but not outmatched. Discipline has prevailed over chaos. And silver, as always, has spoken louder than loyalty.

He paused.

Then added:

Plassey is not a victory of arms alone. It is a victory of position, of perception, of prearranged silence. I have bought a kingdom with less blood than I feared, but at more cost than I can yet see.

Outside, the first carts began rolling in—supplies left behind by fleeing troops, cannon parts, barrels of powder, and boxes of correspondence hastily abandoned in Siraj's tent.
Among the recovered items was a gilded saddlebag stuffed with letters—orders, treaties, and correspondence with French agents.

Clive read them all that evening.

He noted every French name.

Every date.

Every betrayal.

Then he fed them into the campfire, one by one.

By nightfall, Mir Jafar's envoy arrived.

A tall man in ceremonial dress bowed deeply at Clive's tent flap and delivered the message:

"The Nawab is gone. Mir Jafar pledges his loyalty to the Company. He awaits your command."

Clive received the message without standing.

He gave no reply.

Only after the envoy had gone did he take out a fresh sheet of paper, dip his pen again, and write his second message of the night.

This one to Madras.

To the Council,

Bengal is ours. The battle concluded before midday. Mir Jafar has declared himself. I await your instructions as to formal proclamation, but I have already begun arrangements for succession. The fort is secure. The treasury will be counted once the new Nawab is installed.

He signed it with a steady hand:

Robert Clive, Commander of Forces, Bengal Presidency

Then he folded the letter, sealed it, and called for a courier.

As the messenger rode into the night, Clive stood alone in the grove.

The trees around him were quiet again.

But the ground beneath his boots no longer belonged to mangoes.

It belonged to empire.

Chapter 10: The Moment of Betrayal

The battle was fought on a field called Plassey—but the betrayal was born in drawing rooms, behind silk curtains, in whispers carried by silver. It took no oath, no trumpet, no flag to signal its coming. It had only waited for a moment like this.

And now, with Siraj ud-Daulah's army in disarray, it stepped from the shadows.

Mir Jafar stood on the northern ridge of the battlefield, his men arrayed behind him in pristine silence. Their muskets were loaded. Their armor polished. Not a single shot had been fired. They had stood still through the entire storm—watching, calculating, counting.

The message had arrived moments ago.

Clive's courier had ridden hard, sabre notched, face streaked with powder. He delivered only a single line:

"The field is ours. The hour is yours."

Jafar read it once. Then burned it.

Now he faced a choice he had rehearsed in his mind a hundred times: step forward and claim the throne—or do nothing and let history forget him.

His officers surrounded him, waiting.

Some looked anxious. Others eager. All understood what was at stake.

A younger commander broke the silence. "We must move now, my lord. The Nawab has fled."

Jafar looked to the south, where black smoke still rose from the British cannons.

And beyond it, silence.

Siraj was gone.

He turned to his men and gave the order.

"Advance. Raise the white banners. Signal Clive."

Trumpets sounded.

Not the call to war—but the call to allegiance.

Across the field, the Company forces watched the shift in motion.

Kilpatrick was the first to spot it.

"Flags on the north ridge," he called. "They're moving."

Clive raised his spyglass.

He saw them—lines of troops in green and red, hoisting white cloth on tall poles, marching not toward the British lines, but around them—toward Murshidabad.

"Jafar," Clive muttered.

He lowered the glass and nodded once.

"It's done."

There was no cheer.

Just the quiet understanding that power had passed hands not through fire, but through stillness.

Clive ordered a rider to intercept Jafar's vanguard.

"Escort them through the lines. No hostility."

The rider galloped off.

Behind Clive, Coote muttered, "So that's it, then? The betrayal paid for itself."

Clive said nothing.

He walked toward the grove, where wounded sepoys lay resting under mango trees. A young one tried to stand and salute, but Clive waved him down. He picked up a dropped musket and leaned it against the tree. Then he turned back toward the north.

He had just won an empire without a battle cry.

In Murshidabad, the court was in chaos.

The news had traveled faster than any army.

Siraj's chancellor had already fled the palace. Servants tore down his emblems. Merchants burned their ledgers, hoping to conceal past loyalties. The treasury was sealed, the gates bolted, and the ministers waited.

Not for the Nawab.

For the man who had stood still.

Jafar's advance was deliberate.

No looting. No shouting. His troops marched through the city with composure, posting guards at key buildings, disarming Siraj's remaining palace guard, and placing the imperial seal on the treasury.

It took less than a day.

And when Clive arrived the following morning, he found a city already transformed.

Jafar greeted him in the marble courtyard of the palace.

They did not embrace.

They did not smile.

They simply looked at one another—conspirator to kingmaker.

"It is done," Jafar said.

Clive nodded. "Then we begin."

Mir Jafar ascended the throne in silence.

There were no trumpet fanfares, no jubilant crowds, no shower of petals from the palace balconies. Only the solemn beating of drums and the mechanical rhythm of ceremonial words read aloud in Persian, proclaiming him Nawab of Bengal by the will of Allah and the "consent of the people."

The real consent, however, had come from a different source.

Clive stood at the edge of the audience chamber, a guest of honor whose presence overshadowed the entire affair. He did not speak. He did not move. Yet every man in the room—

merchant, minister, priest, and soldier—watched him more than they watched their new Nawab.

Jafar sat beneath the silver canopy, draped in fine muslin and cloth-of-gold. But even in triumph, his expression remained unreadable. He knew what everyone else did: the throne he now occupied had been purchased, not inherited. Secured by a letter, not a sword.

And the debt would soon come due.

That very afternoon, the payments began.

Clive retired to the palace guest wing and summoned Jagat Seth, the powerful financier whose role in the conspiracy had remained discreet but essential. The merchant arrived with two ledgers—one in Bengali, the other in English—and a chest of promissory notes bearing the seal of the new Nawab.

The figures were staggering.

Seventeen million rupees in total.

Three million to the Company for military expenses.

Two million each to British merchants, sepoy commanders, and loyal Indian allies.

Over two million to Clive himself.

The rest—scattered across hundreds of names—bribes, re-wards, hush money.

Clive reviewed the numbers without reaction.
He signed the receipt ledgers, then closed them.
"I'll see the funds moved to Fort William by week's end," Seth said, eyes darting nervously.

Clive nodded. "Make sure it's guarded."

Outside, the streets of Murshidabad murmured with uncertainty. The people did not celebrate Jafar's elevation—they merely adapted to it. Life in Bengal had taught them one thing: power changed hands, but tax remained. Flags changed colors, but famine returned all the same.

Meanwhile, Siraj ud-Daulah fled in disgrace.

He had taken refuge first in a merchant's house, then in a mosque near Rajmahal, disguised as a servant. His loyalists had scattered—some captured, some killed, most surrendered. His treasury was seized, his court disbanded. He was no longer a Nawab. Not even a fugitive king.

Just a boy who had once worn a crown.

Chapter 11: The Pact Fulfilled

The smoke had not yet cleared when the silver was counted.

While bodies were still being dragged from the field at Plassey—sepoys groaning in pain, elephants twitching in the mud, drums still echoing with the rhythm of death—Robert Clive was already preparing for the next war: the war for power.

Siraj ud-Daulah had fled the field in shame, but Bengal did not wait for explanations. Within hours of the Nawab's flight, couriers had galloped ahead to Murshidabad with the news: the

British had won, Siraj was gone, and a new power had emerged from the mango groves.

The court scrambled. Ministers who had once praised Siraj now distanced themselves. Merchants who had financed his armies shifted their loyalties. And in the midst of the chaos, one man stepped forward with studied humility and ruthless timing.

Mir Jafar.

He arrived at Clive's camp the morning after the battle, dressed not as a commander but as a supplicant—bare feet, plain cotton robes, no weapons. But his eyes held calculation, and his entourage followed with the heavy gait of men already assuming power.

Clive received him without ceremony.

The two men—conqueror and kingmaker—faced each other in a stripped-down tent, surrounded only by translators and a single Company clerk recording every word.

Clive began simply. "Is your word still good?"

Jafar nodded. "I did what I promised. Now I will do what you ask."

Clive did not smile. "Then we shall write history together."

The treaty was unrolled on a plain wooden table, its parchment still damp from the river crossing. It had been prepared weeks earlier, signed in secret, and sealed in wax.

Now it was made official.

The East India Company would recognize Mir Jafar as Nawab of Bengal. In return, Jafar would pay the Company seventeen million rupees—split between the army, the naval officers, and Company shareholders. He would also guarantee exclusive trade rights, military cooperation, and legal autonomy for British subjects within Bengal.

It was not a treaty.

It was a purchase.

The Nawabship of Bengal had been bought—not by sword, not by vote, but by accounting.

When the ink dried, Clive extended his hand.
Jafar took it.

The pact was sealed.

But the price was not yet paid.

Over the following weeks, the true scope of the arrangement unfolded.

The Company occupied Fort William fully and permanently. British flags were raised across Calcutta. Merchants who had once dealt only with Bengali agents now paid direct tribute to British officials. Taxes once collected by Mughal-appointed subahdars now flowed into Company treasuries.

And in Murshidabad, the palaces groaned under the weight of coin.

Chests of silver were carried down marble steps by sweating laborers, counted by British clerks under armed guard, and loaded into boats bound for Calcutta.

Clive kept precise accounts.

His own share—over two million rupees—was enough to make him one of the wealthiest men in the empire. It was hush money and hero's pay, bribe and bounty all at once. He accepted it with the cold detachment of a man cashing a check.

He did not spend it.

Not yet.

Instead, he wrote to London.

"We have succeeded beyond measure. Bengal is now secured. The Company shall find its interests well defended under the new Nawab, and peace, I trust, shall reign for a generation."

It was a lie.

Even as the treaty was signed and the coins tallied, Bengal groaned beneath the weight of conquest.

Murshidabad glittered like a jewel.

Its riverfront palaces reflected gold on the Hooghly, domes and minarets piercing the summer haze. Silk merchants shouted in the bazaars, and Persian scribes still whispered poetry in marble halls. But beneath the grandeur, the city trembled. For the first time in memory, it was not the Mughal emperor or his Nawab who ruled Bengal—it was the Company.

And everyone knew it.

Mir Jafar sat on the throne, crowned in emerald and surrounded by the trappings of power. But his eyes flickered nervously with each new petition. He signed edicts with the practiced grace of a veteran officer, but every major decision passed first through Clive's hands or through the watchful eyes of Company advisors stationed just beyond the court.

Clive played the role of honored guest.

He refused to sit on a higher dais than the Nawab. He addressed Jafar in Persian with measured courtesy. He accepted gifts with performative reluctance. But the message was unmistakable: Bengal had a new master—and he wore a red coat.

Yet even victory carried consequences.

The flood of silver nearly drowned the Company's administration. Warehouses overflowed. Coin had to be melted into ingots for transport. A private mint in Calcutta was commissioned just to process the spoils. Meanwhile, London was electrified. East India Company shares soared overnight. Clive's name echoed through Parliament as the "man who had won India with a fraction of her might."

He was offered a barony. He declined.

He didn't need a title. He had Bengal.

But not everyone celebrated.
British officers grumbled that native troops received unequal shares. Indian merchants complained that contracts were voided without compensation. Farmers found their rents increased. And among the Bengali elite, resentment simmered.

Jafar was caught between worlds.

To the British, he was useful. To his own people, he was a traitor. Riots broke out in Burdwan. A grain tax led to unrest near Patna. Religious leaders questioned the Nawab's legitimacy, whispering that a man who came to power through foreign gold could not be the rightful guardian of Bengal.
Jafar appealed to Clive.

"Reduce the demands," he said. "Let the people breathe."

Clive listened. Then tightened the screws.

"The Company has invested much," he replied. "It must see returns."

In the name of security, British troops were stationed permanently in Murshidabad. British judges were placed in Company courts. Trade policies were redrawn to favor British merchants.

When a regional subahdar protested, Clive had him removed—and replaced with a more compliant cousin.

The Nawab watched helplessly.

Even within his own household, loyalty frayed. His eldest son questioned his authority. His ministers wrote letters behind his back. One night, Jafar's chief treasurer was caught trying to flee to the Maratha border with a chest of Company rupees and a map of British troop positions.

Clive dismissed the incident.

"Every empire is born in treason," he said. "The trick is surviving long enough to institutionalize it."

But in quieter moments, even Clive felt the weight of what he had done.

He had turned Bengal into a ledger.

A place where lives and sovereignty were traded like pepper and tea.

One morning, while reviewing troop placements along the Hooghly, he paused at a window and looked out over the river. A funeral procession moved along the banks—locals wading into the shallows, singing in low, mournful tones.

He watched for a long time.

Then returned to the maps.

By the end of July 1757, Bengal had been reordered.
On July 2, Siraj was captured.

Clive was informed by dispatch just before dawn. The messenger did not need to say what came next.

By midday, Siraj was dead.

Killed by soldiers loyal to Jafar, under pretext of "preventing further disorder." No trial. No proclamation. Just a blade in a locked room, and a shallow grave beneath the neem trees outside the city walls.

Clive did not protest.

He did not approve either.

He simply moved on.

In the following days, he met with Jafar regularly, guiding the first acts of the new regime. Trade monopolies were redrawn. British customs privileges were expanded. A permanent garrison of Company troops was granted rights to occupy key posts in Calcutta, Cossimbazar, and Patna.

When Jafar hesitated at one proposal, Clive reminded him:

"You owe the throne to our silence, not just our steel."

The new Nawab nodded.

And signed.

On July 10, Clive sent a letter to London.

It was brief.

"The situation in Bengal has stabilized. A friendly government is in place. Revenue will increase by the next season. The East India Company's position is now unassailable."

He didn't mention Siraj.

He didn't mention the field of Plassey.

He didn't mention the blood.

Instead, he enclosed a separate package—a golden bracelet from Jafar, set with rubies, symbolizing their alliance. It was a gift, and a message.

Clive wrote one additional note to accompany it:

"The Emperor of Delhi grants titles. The Nawab of Bengal grants favors. But it is the Company that holds the future."

Mir Jafar ruled in name.

But it was Clive who held the reins.

And now that Bengal had been secured, the Company turned its eyes elsewhere—toward Bihar, Orissa, and the Ganges plain beyond.

Empire was addictive.

And this was only the beginning.

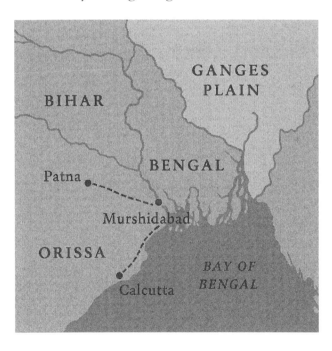

Chapter 12: The Gates of Plassey

Victory at Plassey had broken the back of the Nawab's army, but it had not broken the spirit of resistance in Bengal.

In the weeks that followed Siraj's defeat and execution, Clive's forces remained on constant alert. Mutiny was whispered in every garrison. The countryside rippled with unrest. Rumors spread of scattered bands of Siraj's loyalists regrouping in the north, of Maratha agents slipping across the frontier, of French operatives stirring rebellion among the zamindars.

The gates of Plassey, metaphorical and real, were not yet secure.

Clive knew it.

He moved quickly to lock them shut.

The mango groves, still scarred by cannon fire and littered with broken carts and rusting sabers, were cleared by native laborers under British guard. The battlefield itself became a symbol—

Clive ordered a simple marker placed at the center of the grove, inscribed with the date and a brief phrase in Persian:

"The day the tide turned."

But for many in Bengal, the tide had not turned—it had pulled away and left devastation in its wake.

Clive established a fortified cantonment near Plassey with British sepoy companies garrisoned under rotating command. He appointed his most trusted officers to oversee tax collection in the region, bypassing the Nawab's own officials. Revenue began to flow directly to the Company.

This wasn't occupation. It was absorption.

The political consequences came fast.

Local rulers, once nominally loyal to Murshidabad, now sent tributes directly to Calcutta. Merchant guilds, unsure whom to trust, began paying British customs agents in advance. Religious leaders, pressured by the shifting balance of power, sent envoys to Fort William offering blessings—and asking for protection.

The Nawab, humiliated in his own capital, became a recluse.

Mir Jafar's court shrank.

He stopped holding public audiences. He grew suspicious of his own ministers. His letters to Clive became longer, more desperate—requests for guidance, demands for assurances, pleas for British officers to remain close "for counsel."

Clive obliged—but on his terms.

He began to see what Bengal could become—not just a puppet state, but a launchpad. A beachhead from which British power could expand across the subcontinent. If Bengal could fall so quickly, so completely, why not Bihar? Why not Awadh? Why not the whole of Hindustan?

He wasn't alone in thinking this.

Letters arrived from London, filled with praise and caution in equal measure. The Company's board of directors congratulated him for restoring order and restoring profit—always profit—but warned him not to overreach. There were treaties to consider. European eyes watching. Parliament would not sanction imperial expansion—at least not openly.

Clive ignored them.

He understood what the board did not: the empire was already here.

It wore no crown. It flew no flag. It marched in the margins of contracts and treaties. But it was real. And it was growing.

Meanwhile, the Nawab's enemies stirred.

Across the northern plain, scattered officers from Siraj's army refused to accept Jafar's rule. One of his cousins, a fiery commander named Khuda Yar Khan, raised a militia near Rajmahal and declared Siraj's death a British fabrication. He claimed the true Nawab still lived, hidden, and would soon return to drive the Company into the sea.

Clive dispatched a column of sepoys to crush the rebellion. They moved swiftly, with artillery and cavalry support. The rebel camp was torched, its leaders captured and hanged by the roadside. A message was nailed to the charred gates:

"Betrayal is a currency. You will not spend it twice."

But the skirmish unnerved Clive.

He began to see shadows in every quiet village, every troop movement. His military instincts sharpened into paranoia. He doubled guard rotations in Calcutta. He had the outer walls of Fort William reinforced. He sent agents posing as traders to Murshidabad and Patna, tasked with reporting on local sentiment.

One such report came from a Company spy embedded in Jafar's own palace.

It read: *"The Nawab speaks of retirement. His son whispers of restoration. The court speaks only in riddles and curses."*

Clive read it, then folded it neatly and burned it.

He began drawing up plans.

If Jafar faltered—he would need a replacement.

By August of 1757, the illusion of stability was beginning to crack.

Murshidabad had become a city of silences—ministers who no longer spoke in full sentences, palace corridors once bustling with clerks now empty, and Mir Jafar himself reduced to muttering anxiously during Council sessions. He still wore the crown, but it had become too heavy.

He summoned Clive for a private audience.

They met in a shaded pavilion overlooking the Bhagirathi River. The Nawab arrived late, dressed in his ceremonial robes but without his usual escort. He seemed smaller than before, hunched slightly, as though age had crept in all at once.

"You must help me," Jafar said, skipping all pleasantries. "The court is against me. My own household no longer obeys."

Clive said nothing at first. He let the words sit in the warm air.

Then he asked, "Do you intend to abdicate?"

Jafar looked away. "I do not know."

"If you do," Clive said carefully, "you must name a successor. And he must not be your son."

Jafar's face darkened. "You fear a boy with ambition?"

"I fear a boy with nothing to lose."

There was a long pause. The Nawab's fingers trembled slightly as he adjusted his sash. "What would you have me do?"

Clive stood, his voice low and deliberate. "Keep the peace.

Collect the taxes. Smile. That is all we ask."

He left the pavilion without waiting for dismissal.

Back in Calcutta, Clive began preparations for what he increasingly believed was inevitable: regime change.

His agents compiled dossiers on potential replacements—minor nobles, rival generals, even distant cousins of the Mughal emperor. Each candidate was judged not by lineage or piety, but by three criteria: their loyalty, their debt, and their fear.

But for the moment, Jafar still served a purpose.

And so Clive pressed forward with his real work—remaking Bengal's machinery.

Revenue collection was consolidated under Company oversight. A new customs system was introduced that effectively exempted British merchants from any meaningful taxation. Courts previously operated under Persianate legal codes were now instructed to favor Company interests. British officers began wearing local garb in public to mask their growing control, a tactic Clive called "dignified invisibility."

And all the while, he watched.

He watched who came and went from Murshidabad.

He watched the flow of grain and coin.

He watched his own officers for signs of disloyalty.

There was one in particular—Major Kilpatrick—whose ambition had begun to show through the cracks of his obedience.

Clive noted it, then offered him a new assignment in the distant hill country. A reward, he said. Kilpatrick accepted, and Clive replaced him with someone hungrier for approval.
Even in victory, Clive trusted few.

In September, a letter arrived from Madras. It was terse and formal. The Company directors, while impressed by his results, expressed concern over his "unofficial decisions," particularly the elevation of Jafar without London's prior sanction. Clive read the letter twice, then scrawled a reply:

"I did not wait for London's approval because Bengal would not wait for London's delay."

He knew how slowly London moved. And he knew how quickly Bengal could unravel.

The same week, another message reached Fort William—from a merchant caravan en route from Patna. It reported signs of unrest among the Afghani traders near the northwest border.

Small villages looted. Tax collectors killed.

Clive closed the letter and handed it to his secretary.

"Alert General Coote," he said. "Double the patrols west of Rajshahi. And tell the Nawab—quietly—that he will not need to respond. We will handle it."

The message was clear.

Jafar could keep the crown.

But Clive held the kingdom.

Chapter 13: Collapse

It did not take long for the cracks to appear.

Mir Jafar sat on a throne, but the seat was hollow. His palace echoed with footsteps he didn't trust. His ministers bowed deeply but whispered behind his back. The army that had once followed him with deference now eyed him with suspicion. Even the court poets grew quiet—what praise could be offered to a man crowned by foreigners?

He had everything he wanted.

And nothing he could hold.

Barely a month after the Battle of Plassey, the new Nawab of Bengal found himself isolated within the marble halls of Murshidabad. The British had left behind a regiment of sepoys to "advise and assist," but Jafar knew better. They weren't advisors. They were watchers.

Clive had returned to Calcutta, taking with him the real power.

In his absence, Company agents began swarming the court like locusts. Every contract renegotiated. Every tax route revised. British traders now operated with full exemption from customs. Indian merchants were sidelined. Company-appointed clerks reviewed the Nawab's treasury books. When Jafar objected, he was reminded of the payments still owed.

Clive, in his letters, remained cordial but firm.

"Our shared success requires stability," he wrote. **"Stability requires order. And order, I am sure Your Highness will agree, is best maintained with transparency."**
"Transparency" meant forfeiture.

By late August, the Nawab no longer issued orders without Company consultation. His own generals answered first to British officers. His revenue ministers, chosen in negotiation with Clive, prioritized remittances to Fort William before addressing the provincial coffers.

Jafar's courtiers grew uneasy.

His family resentful.

And his subjects restless.

In the countryside, the effects were immediate.

Taxes were raised to fund the massive payout to the Company. Landlords, under pressure, squeezed tenant farmers. Grain prices surged. Small zamindars, unable to pay, lost their holdings to Company-aligned rivals. Even routine festivals became subdued—music quieted, offerings fewer, temples starved of donation.

A famine loomed—not yet of food, but of faith.

Meanwhile, rumors spread of conspiracies.

Not against Clive.

But against Jafar.

One morning, a palace guard confessed under duress that he had been approached by agents of a rival noble house offering gold to smuggle weapons into the city. Two of the Nawab's cousins were caught intercepting a Company convoy carrying silver from Patna. The convoy was untouched. But the message was clear.

The throne was contested.

Clive returned to Murshidabad in early September, summoned by a flurry of letters marked urgent. He arrived unannounced, with only a small retinue, and went directly to the palace.

Jafar received him in a private chamber, dressed not in royal finery but in plain white linen.

"I need help," the Nawab said before formalities were exchanged.

Clive studied him.

The man before him was thinner, greyer, eyes sunken from sleeplessness. His hands trembled slightly as he reached for a cup of water.

"The people curse me," Jafar continued. "The court ignores me. My own son does not speak in my presence. What would you have me do?"

Clive remained silent for a long moment.

Then, with the calm of a man confirming something already decided, he said:

"You will maintain order. You will fulfill your obligations.

And you will do so with our guidance."

"And if I cannot?" Jafar asked.

Clive leaned forward. "Then we will find one who can."

Jafar looked down.

He said nothing.

Clive rose.

He left the chamber without bowing.
That night, he wrote three letters.

One to Fort William, requesting additional Company officers to oversee tax collection.

One to London, confirming that Bengal remained "aligned and profitable."

And one to a man named Miran—Jafar's son.

It read:

"The future of Bengal lies in steady hands. Let us speak soon about your readiness to lead."

Miran opened Clive's letter with shaking hands.
He was barely twenty—ambitious, impatient, and burning with the same quiet fury that had once consumed his father.

But where Jafar hesitated, Miran acted. He had spent the weeks following Plassey maneuvering in the shadows: cultivating allies, bribing ministers, and studying Clive's methods with the eye of a student and the hunger of a rival.

Now, with a single page of elegant English script, the door had been opened.

The letter was brief, but unmistakable in its intent.

Clive was testing him.

And Miran meant to pass.

In the days that followed, the young prince increased his influence. He took over military reviews from his father, appearing in public in full regalia—plumed turban, jeweled saber, surrounded by handpicked cavalry. He issued edicts on Jafar's behalf. He negotiated with Company officers directly, bypassing the Nawab's court entirely.

Clive, still in Murshidabad, watched carefully.

He met privately with Miran twice—once in the gardens of the old palace, and once in the Company's fortified house along the Bhagirathi. Neither meeting was announced. No minutes were kept. But word of them spread fast.

And Jafar noticed.

He summoned Clive for a formal audience.

When the Company delegation arrived, the court chamber was nearly empty. Only a handful of ministers stood along the walls, and the Nawab himself sat rigid, eyes heavy with suspicion.

"You speak with my son," Jafar said without preamble.

Clive inclined his head. "I speak with many who have the future of Bengal in mind."

"I am not dead," the Nawab replied.

"Then rule like it," Clive said.

A long silence followed.

Finally, Jafar slumped in his seat. "What would you have me do?"

Clive didn't answer directly.
Instead, he rose.

"This is your kingdom, Highness. But your crown was paid for with more than gold. You must govern not just in name—but in deed. Or your son will."

He turned and left.

Jafar didn't stop him.

That evening, the Nawab dismissed several long-serving ministers—including one who had been with him since Siraj's court. The message was clear: he would try to reclaim authority. But it was too late.

The collapse had already begun.

Outside the palace, resentment simmered.

The peasantry faced new taxes. Merchants grumbled that British exemptions were strangling trade. Temple priests complained that Company reforms threatened their authority.

Even zamindars—once happy to collect rents for the crown—now whispered that they were being bypassed entirely by English agents.

Clive's solution was ruthless: restructure.

He installed Company "residencies" in key cities—miniature administrations that monitored local governance under the guise of partnership. These officers—often young, ambitious, and utterly loyal—reported directly to Fort William. They advised local rulers, oversaw tax policy, and "supported" judicial reform.

But everyone knew the truth.
Bengal no longer belonged to the Nawab.

It belonged to the Company.

Clive returned to Calcutta by October, leaving behind a province in crisis—but a ledger in perfect balance. Profits were up. Smuggling had been reduced. Military posts were secure.

And Mir Jafar remained, for now, on the throne.

But Clive knew it was temporary.

He had begun drafting options for replacement.

Miran was only one possibility.

There were others—nobles with ambition, generals with grievances, younger sons of older dynasties eager to rise.
What mattered was loyalty. What mattered was predictability.

What mattered was that Bengal continued to produce silver, not surprises.

In one of his final letters from Murshidabad, Clive wrote:

"The governance of Bengal cannot rest on ceremony. It must rest on structure. And that structure must be ours."

He left no room for debate.

Jafar was now a placeholder.

And the Company no longer needed placeholders.

Siraj fled the battlefield as swiftly as his broken pride would carry him, discarding his royal robes for common garb and vanishing into the countryside. But betrayal travels faster than loyalty.

It was not long before Mir Jafar's men, the very hands that once swore fealty to the Nawab, captured him near Rajmahal. Brought back to Murshidabad under guard, Siraj was summarily executed—stabbed in the chest and left in an unmarked grave.

There would be no funeral, no elegy. Only silence.

His death marked not just the fall of a man, but the death knell of independent Benga

Chapter 14: Victory Without Glory

Victory, however, was just the beginning. The Company had not come to govern—it had come to profit. What followed was not reconstruction, but extraction. Bengal was no longer a kingdom but a balance sheet. Its fertile plains, once thick with rice and mustard, were converted into taxable plots, their yields funneled toward London.

Revenue, not reform, became the order of the day. The Company counted its spoils, and the people counted their losses.

Robert Clive returned to Calcutta not in triumph, but in calculation.

The road from Murshidabad was lined with uneasy onlookers—merchants, farmers, Brahmin priests, and clerks from broken courts. Some bowed. Some looked away. None cheered. The conqueror of Bengal passed them in silence, seated atop a horse draped in modest cloth, his officers following in a line more functional than regal.

He had won.

But no victory march could disguise what had been traded for the crown.

In the weeks since Plassey, Clive had consolidated British authority with military efficiency. Fort William now served as the unofficial capital of British India, not merely a trading post but a seat of governance. From its shaded halls, decisions were made about taxation, infrastructure, justice—and, increasingly, the future of the subcontinent.

But even Clive could feel the weight pressing in.

Every message from London praised the profits but questioned the methods.

Every letter from Company directors was double-edged: *Excellent revenues—but do ensure local sentiment remains manageable. Secure trade—but refrain from overt domination.*

They wanted an empire.

But they wanted it politely.

Clive, in his private journals, was blunt.

"They want a palace without paying the architect. They want a garden where I've just finished digging a trench."

He had never trusted Parliament. He trusted the Company even less.

Back in Calcutta, Clive set to work formalizing what had already happened. Committees were formed. Trade licenses were rewritten. Company officers were given broader mandates. The "Plassey Fund," financed by Mir Jafar's payouts, was disbursed to cover military costs and future administrative expenses.

And then came the reward.

On December 10, 1757, Clive received a packet from London.

Inside: his formal commission as Governor of the Presidency of Fort William, ratified by the Court of Directors and carrying with it expanded powers over the Bengal territories.

He read it in silence.

Then burned the envelope.

He knew what it meant.

They were tying him to the chair he had already taken.

That evening, he walked alone through the gardens of the Governor's House. The palms swayed gently in the winter breeze. The Hooghly River shimmered under moonlight. It was quiet—the kind of quiet he had never known in England, nor on the battlefield.

And yet, he felt no peace.

A steward approached. "Sir, the council is ready for tomorrow's review."

Clive nodded. "Have them bring the treasury ledgers. And the tax rolls. We'll begin with the salt routes."

Salt.

Not glory. Not strategy.

Salt.

He returned inside and sat at his desk.

Opened a drawer.

Removed a small cloth pouch.

Inside was a ring—heavy, engraved with the arms of the Nawab. A gift from Jafar, intended to symbolize their "eternal alliance."

Clive turned it in his hand, then placed it beside his inkstand.

He never wore it.

The spoils were vast. The silence, vaster still.

In the months following the Battle of Plassey, Clive's fortune soared. He was now one of the richest men in the British Empire—not by inheritance, not through invention, but by conquest rendered with a merchant's quill. Seventeen million rupees had flowed from Murshidabad into the Company's ledgers, and nearly two of those million had gone directly into

Clive's personal accounts.

But with wealth came scrutiny.

Whispers grew louder in the corridors of London's East India House. Clive's name was praised in the quarterly reports—always just after a line about irregular disbursements, excessive rewards, or "unorthodox political arrangements." Behind the numbers, the directors smelled danger.

He was too successful.

Too independent.

Too visible.

Clive knew it. And he didn't care.

He had learned long ago that empires were built not with perfect records, but with undeniable results. The Company's share price had doubled. Trade routes were secure. Bengal's revenues dwarfed those of Madras and Bombay combined.
Let them grumble in their clubs and counting houses. He had delivered what they could only imagine.

But something in him was shifting.

He no longer roamed the forts as he once had. He no longer stood among the sepoys or dined with junior officers. His circle narrowed—older, colder, populated by advisors and accountants. He spent long hours in his study, reviewing shipping manifests, customs reports, and affidavits from zamindars whose names he would never learn to pronounce.

Sometimes, he would pause.

Stare at the maps.

At Bengal.
At Plassey.

He began to write less in his journals.

And when he did, it was different.

"I have made a king, but not a friend."

"The Company now has a crown, but no soul."

"I wonder who will hold the pen when the reckoning comes."

Still, he worked.

Still, he planned.

His final major act as Governor before returning to England was to secure a new system of dual administration—whereby Indian officials nominally retained their positions, but were overseen by Company officers with real authority. It was elegant. Efficient. Absolute.

No more need for puppet Nawabs.

Just a machine.

A colonial engine dressed in native robes.

When the system was implemented, Clive gave no speech.

He simply issued the orders and returned to his office. Later that week, an officer asked him if he felt proud.

Clive had looked up from his papers and said: "Proud? I feel nothing at all."

By March 1760, his decision was made.

He would return to England.

Not to rest—but to report.

To reshape the narrative before it reshaped him.

He left Fort William the same way he had arrived years earlier: unsmiling, determined, dragging behind him a ledger too large for the ship's cabin and a name too heavy for the Crown to ignore.

His final act in India was private.

He visited the mango grove at Plassey.
Alone.

No escort. No fanfare.

He walked the field where cannon smoke had once obscured the sun. The trees had regrown. The ground, once gouged by wheels and hooves and bodies, was flat again.

But he remembered it all.

Where the center had nearly broken.

Where Madan had died.

Where Mir Jafar's troops had stood still.

He knelt once, not in reverence, but in reflection.

Then he stood.

And turned his back on the field.

Chapter 15: The Empire Consumes Its Maker

Victory, however, was just the beginning. What followed was not reconstruction—but extraction. Bengal became a ledger entry, its fields turned into coin.

Robert Clive once believed that empire was a matter of will. That a sharp mind, a steady hand, and a strong sword could bend history toward order. That power, properly managed, could serve both profit and principle. But in the cold, gas-lit drawing rooms of London, Clive discovered something far more dangerous than Nawabs, sepoys, or jungle rebellions:

The empire had a mind of its own.

By 1769, two years after his final return from India, Clive was a man unmoored. His estates in Shropshire were quiet, meticulously kept, and utterly empty of purpose. He hosted few guests, ignored invitations, and walked his grounds in silence.

The grandeur of Walcot Hall had faded into routine. The silk from Bengal no longer shimmered. The map over the fireplace felt less like a trophy and more like a tombstone.

And the newspapers would not stop.

Each week brought a new pamphlet, a new cartoon, a new accusation. One showed him stuffing Indian children into moneybags. Another portrayed him strangling the Nawab with a ledger. Satirists turned "Plassey" into a punchline. In Parliament, the so-called "India Inquiry" dragged his name across the coals.

He was accused of extortion. Of treason. Of crimes against the Company, the Crown, and humanity itself.

None of it stuck.

But all of it scarred.

Clive defended himself with precision and ferocity. In a speech before the House of Commons in 1772, he recounted his actions in Bengal line by line, citing dates, witnesses, and revenues. His voice never wavered. His logic never failed.

The chamber fell silent as he closed:

"I fought your battles. I won your empire. And now you shrink from the consequences of your own conquest. Gentlemen, I stand astonished at my own moderation."

It was a masterstroke. The inquiry collapsed.

But the damage was done.

He had become a cautionary tale.

The Company distanced itself. New policies restricted officer conduct abroad—"Clive's Law," they called them. The Crown seized greater authority over India, slowly transforming Company holdings into de facto colonies. The British public, once thrilled by conquest, now recoiled at the price.

Clive, once the lion, had become the scapegoat.

His health worsened. The old war wounds ached. Fevers came and went. His addiction to laudanum deepened. He grew paranoid—checking the locks on his doors, rereading letters for imagined threats. Friends visited less frequently. Margaret remained dutiful but distant.

In his journals, his handwriting grew erratic.

"The price of greatness," he wrote, "is that you outlive your usefulness."

Yet there were moments—brief, electric moments—when the fire returned.

When a visiting officer asked him how he had taken Plassey with so few men, Clive smiled for the first time in days.

"I didn't take it," he said. "I bought it. I paid in silver. In ink. In trust betrayed."

And then, after a pause: "And it cost more than any battle I ever fought."

In 1774, Parliament offered him a new commission—symbolic, mostly. A way to placate the old lion. He declined.

That same year, the famine in Bengal reached London in newsprint. One-third of the population dead. Crops failed. The Company blamed nature. Reformers blamed Clive.

He said nothing.

He no longer believed that history was written by the victors.

It was written by survivors.

By the autumn of 1774, Robert Clive was a man consumed by the very forces he had unleashed.

The East India Company—his creation, his battlefield, his crown—had grown into something monstrous. Its profits soared, but its soul withered. Villages in Bengal were left to rot while London investors counted dividends. The famine that had claimed millions was buried beneath balance sheets. The same boardrooms that once toasted his name now whispered that he had gone too far.

He agreed.

But he also knew he'd done what they never had the stomach to do.

Mir Jafar took the throne as promised—but sovereignty meant little with Clive in his court and Company agents watching his treasury. He soon learned what it meant to wear a crown not forged by loyalty, but by debt.

Jagat Seth, the banker behind the plot, was rewarded handsomely—but uneasily. He knew better than most that those who fund kings often become their hostages.

Clive withdrew further into solitude. His estates, though expansive, felt like a prison. He wandered the halls of Walcot Hall at night, trailing his fingers along carved balustrades from Murshidabad. In his study, he sat for hours staring at maps, now outdated, the borders of India shifting again beyond his control.

He rarely slept.

When he did, the dreams returned—mango groves soaked in blood, elephants fleeing cannon fire, Siraj's wild eyes in the smoke at Plassey. He would wake with clenched fists and a racing heart, drenched in sweat, reaching for his laudanum before he even opened his eyes.

Physicians came and went. So did friends.

He became short with his wife, then distant. His sons, now young men, tried to understand the fire behind their father's silence, but it was no use. He was a man from another world— a world he had built, then watched turn to ash.

On November 22, 1774, he dressed in silence.

He wore his best coat. The one from India.

He sat at his desk. Wrote no letter. Made no speech.

Then he locked the door.

He was found hours later, a blade beside him, a small bottle of laudanum shattered on the floor. Whether the final blow had been made by hand or poison, the inquest never said with certainty. The cause was listed, delicately, as *an illness of the mind.*

The newspapers were more direct.

"Clive, the Conqueror of India, Dead by His Own Hand."

In Parliament, a few members rose to offer praise. Most remained seated.

But far away, in the courtyards of Murshidabad, in the bazaars of Calcutta, in the fading memory of those who had survived the Black Hole, Arcot, and Plassey—his name lived on.

A name that stirred pride in some, fury in others, and fear in all.

Because Robert Clive had not merely changed India.

He had changed the British Empire.

He had shown that conquest could be executed not just with steel, but with contracts.

That power could be seized not only through battle—but through betrayal, balance sheets, and bureaucratic will.

He had proven that a single man, if bold enough, could carve a kingdom out of chaos.
And he had paid the price.

Not in rupees.

Not in honor.

But in peace.

Chapter 16: Epilogue – The Shadow of Plassey

Plassey never ended.

It echoed—not just in the halls of Fort William or the court of Murshidabad, but across the entire structure of the British Empire. What Clive began in 1757 did not stop with Bengal. It expanded, metastasized, and hardened into a system that would define the next two centuries.

In the years following Clive's death, the East India Company tightened its grip. His reforms, once controversial, became precedent. His tactics—manipulation of local rulers, strategic betrayal, economic subjugation—were taught, studied, replicated.

By the turn of the 19th century, the Company no longer just traded in India.

It *ruled* it.

The Diwani rights granted to Clive were only the beginning.

Within decades, the Company's army outnumbered the British Army itself. From the Punjab to the Deccan, from Sindh to Assam, regional powers were absorbed, disarmed, or destroyed. Treaties were rewritten with British ink. Laws were passed in languages never spoken by those they governed.

And always, in the background, was Plassey.

The blueprint.

The justification.

The origin myth of imperial India.

In London, Clive's reputation swung like a pendulum. At times he was venerated—his portrait hung in the National Gallery, his campaigns cited in textbooks, his wealth romanticized. At other times, he was reviled—a symbol of colonial greed, of moral decay, of the dark bargain between commerce and conquest.

His estate at Walcot fell into decline. Visitors to his tomb debated whether to lay flowers or curses. Statues erected in his honor would, in time, be defaced. His name remained on plaques and street signs, but also in debates about empire, ethics, and reparations.

In India, his legacy was sharper still.

For generations, children in Bengal were taught his name not as a hero, but as a herald of ruin. The famine of 1770, which followed his reforms, killed nearly ten million. The native nobility he had co-opted collapsed under the weight of Company corruption. Artisans once protected by Mughal courts were taxed into extinction. Entire regions were reshaped not by culture or language, but by trade routes and British law.

Yet Clive did not see this future.

He saw only his own ambition.

The need to prove himself, to rise above a world that had dismissed him, beaten him, tried to forget him. His greatest conquest, in truth, had never been India.

It had been *England*.

He forced a nation to reckon with its own hypocrisy—its hunger for power hidden behind silks and sermons. He gave it empire, and in return, it gave him exile.

But the seeds he planted continued to grow.

The Raj. The Mutiny. The Viceroys. The railroads, the salt tax, the partition of Bengal. All of it—each decision, each act of oppression and resistance—traced back to a grove of mango trees on the morning of June 23, 1757.

Plassey was never just a battle.

It was the moment the British stopped pretending they came to India to trade—and began admitting they had come to rule.

Two centuries after Robert Clive's victory beneath the mango trees, the British Empire stood at its zenith.

Red stretched across the globe—across deserts, mountains, and seas. India, the so-called "jewel in the crown," had become the administrative heart of a global system. Railroads stitched together provinces. Telegraph wires crackled across thousands of miles. Governors, dressed in white linen and confidence, sat in marble halls built on the bones of forgotten kingdoms.

But the foundation was never stable.

Because the foundation was Plassey.

The conquest had not been spiritual or civilizational—it had been financial. Tactical. Opportunistic. And the Indian people had never forgotten.

In 1857, a century after Clive's campaign, Bengal exploded again.

The Sepoy Mutiny—or the First War of Independence, as it would later be known—erupted from the barracks of Meerut and spread like fire across the subcontinent. British officers were killed in their homes. Native regiments defected. Old princely states declared rebellion.

At the heart of the uprising was a deep memory: of betrayal, exploitation, and a government that had never governed for the people, only for profit.

Plassey was invoked again and again.

The rebellion failed—but it shattered the illusion of invincibility. The East India Company was dissolved in disgrace. Rule passed directly to the British Crown, and Queen Victoria was proclaimed Empress of India.

But even under imperial robes, the old model remained. Control through division. Rule through commerce. Conquest by accounting.

The 20th century brought new voices.

Gandhi, Nehru, Bose. Movements that refused to bow. Salt marches, boycotts, hunger strikes. A rebellion not of armies, but of the soul. And always, behind the speeches and slogans, behind the push for independence, was a long shadow:

The understanding that what had begun in a bribe, a letter, a quiet betrayal—could not be allowed to last forever.

On August 15, 1947, the Union Jack was lowered across India for the final time.

The empire Clive had helped build cracked apart.
Partition followed. Bloodshed. Division. But also freedom.

In Murshidabad, the palaces stood still. Tourists passed through rooms once filled with whispers. In the old mango grove at Plassey, a monument was erected—not grand, not imperial, just a simple white stone bearing the date.

Bengali schoolchildren walk past it now on field trips.

Some pause. Some don't.

But the earth still remembers.

It remembers cannon fire and broken promises. It remembers how a foreign company came to trade and stayed to rule. It remembers a man from Shropshire who arrived with nothing and left with a nation in his pocket.

And somewhere in the silent breeze that moves through the trees, it still echoes:

This is where it began.

Not with a declaration.

Not with a war.

But with a choice.

A signature.

And a silence that thundered for centuries.

Flag of the East India Trading Company

Logo of the East India Trading Company

Mughal imperial banne

The Banner of Siraj ud-Daulah

APPENDIX A: Time line of Events

PRELUDE TO PLASSEY

1600 – The British East India Company is founded by royal charter to pursue trade in the East Indies.

1690 – British establish a trading post at Calcutta, later fortified and expanded into Fort William.

1756 (June) – Siraj ud-Daulah becomes Nawab of Bengal and demands British dismantle Fort William's defenses.

1756 (June 20) – Siraj captures Fort William; 123 British prisoners die in the "Black Hole of Calcutta" (controversial account).

1756 (December) – Robert Clive arrives from Madras with Company reinforcements to retake Calcutta.

1757 (January) – British retake Calcutta. Tensions rise as Clive prepares a campaign to unseat Siraj.

1757 (Spring) – Secret negotiations begin with Mir Jafar, promising him the Nawabship in exchange for betrayal.

1757 (June 23) – **Battle of Plassey**: Clive's 3,000 men defeat Siraj's 50,000-strong army due to betrayal and discipline. Siraj flees and is captured and executed.

THE RISE OF THE EAST INDIA COMPANY (1757–1857)

1757–1765 – Mir Jafar becomes Nawab, but power remains with the Company. Clive becomes extremely wealthy.

1760 – Clive returns to England, hailed as a hero.

1764 – Battle of Buxar further cements Company military superiority in India.

1765 – The Mughal Emperor grants the Company *diwani* rights to collect revenue in Bengal, Bihar, and Orissa.

1770 – The Bengal Famine kills 10 million; Company policies blamed.

1774 – Clive dies by suicide amid scandal and public inquiry.

1790s–1830s – The Company expands across India, conquering Mysore, Maratha Confederacy, and Sikh Empire.

1835 – English made the official language of administration and education in India.

1856 – Lord Dalhousie's "Doctrine of Lapse" annexes Indian princely states without heirs, angering elites.

THE 1857 REBELLION & BRITISH RAJ (1857–1947)

1857 (May) – The **Indian Rebellion of 1857** begins among Company sepoys; spreads across North India.

1858 – The British Crown abolishes the East India Company. India becomes a formal colony under the **British Raj**.

1876 – Queen Victoria is declared *Empress of India*.

1885 – The Indian National Congress (INC) is formed to advocate for Indian rights.

1905 – First partition of Bengal sparks protests; British reverse decision in 1911.

1919 – Amritsar Massacre: British troops kill hundreds of peaceful protesters, galvanizing anti-colonial movements.

1920s–1930s – **Mahatma Gandhi** leads nonviolent campaigns: the Salt March, civil disobedience, and boycott of British goods.

1942 – "Quit India Movement" demands full British withdrawal.

1947 (August 15) – **India gains independence**, but is partitioned into India and Pakistan, triggering mass violence and displacement.

POST-COLONIAL LEGACY (1947–Present)

1950 – India becomes a secular republic with a democratic constitution.

1971 – Bangladesh (formerly East Pakistan) gains independence.

1997 – The 50th anniversary of Indian independence sparks global reassessment of the British Empire's legacy.

2007 – Britain marks the 250th anniversary of the Battle of Plassey; Indian scholars and activists challenge its colonial framing.

2010s–2020s – Renewed calls in Britain and India for historical reckoning, reparations, and decolonizing the curriculum.

Today – Plassey remains a symbol of both imperial cunning and national trauma—its legacy deeply woven into the histories of India, Britain, and global capitalism.

The Plassey Mango Grove as it looks today

Appendix B: What is a Nabob?

What Is a Nabob?

The term *nabob* originally comes from the Urdu word *naib* or *nawab*, a title used for regional rulers or governors under the Mughal Empire in India. When British East India Company officials began gaining immense wealth and influence during the 18th century—especially through political manipulation and commercial dominance in India—the term was ironically repurposed back in Britain to describe those who returned home with vast fortunes.

A *nabob* came to signify a British man who had enriched himself in India, often through questionable means, and who now wielded outsized social and political influence back in England.

It carried a tone of both admiration and disdain—admired for his wealth, distrusted for its origins.

Clive and the Rise of the Nabobs

Robert Clive is perhaps the most iconic *nabob* in British history. After orchestrating the British victory at the Battle of Plassey in 1757, Clive returned to Britain with unimaginable riches, earning titles, political clout, and the scrutiny of Parliament.

Though hailed as a hero by some, he was vilified by others as the epitome of colonial greed and corruption.

Clive's role in establishing Company rule over Bengal—and enriching himself in the process—cemented the *nabob* as a symbol of the East India Company's moral ambiguities. His legacy embodies the tension between empire-building and profiteering, ambition and exploitation, heroism and hubris.

Historical and Archaic Variants:
- Nawab
  The original Persian/Urdu word a title of provincial governors under the Mughal Empire. Still used in Indian contexts.
- Naib
  A related root form in Arabic and Persian meaning "deputy" or "viceroy."
- Nabob *(Anglicized form)*
  Adopted by the British in the 17th–18th centuries to describe wealthy East India Company men who returned to England with enormous fortunes.

Less Common / Outdated:
- Naubob or Nawbob
  Occasionally found in 18th-century British satire or phonetic transcriptions but largely obsolete today.

Meaning in British English:

In British usage, especially in the 18th and 19th centuries, a "nabob" referred to a British man who made a fortune in India and returned home wealthy — often seen as ostentatious or morally compromised by their sudden rise. The term was frequently used with irony or suspicion in political and social commentary.

Appendix C: Major Characters

Robert Clive (Clive of India)

A former clerk turned military commander, Robert Clive rose through the ranks of the British East India Company with a mix of daring, strategic brilliance, and ruthless pragmatism. At the Battle of Plassey in 1757, he orchestrated a decisive and world-changing victory that allowed the Company to take control of Bengal. His legacy is deeply controversial—seen as both a founding figure of the British Empire and a symbol of colonial exploitation.

Siraj ud-Daulah

The young, impetuous Nawab of Bengal, Siraj ud-Daulah was only 18 when he inherited the throne in 1756. Fiercely protective of his sovereignty, he clashed with the East India Company over fortifications in Calcutta and ultimately led his army against Clive at Plassey. His defeat marked the beginning of British dominion in India, and his tragic downfall epitomized the cost of internal betrayal.

Mir Jafar

A senior commander in Siraj's army, Mir Jafar was instrumental in the British victory at Plassey—not by fighting, but by standing still. Secretly promised the throne in exchange for his neutrality, he betrayed the Nawab during the battle. Though he became Nawab afterward, he quickly found himself powerless under British control.

Eyre Coote

A loyal and competent officer under Clive's command, Eyre Coote played a critical role in organizing British forces during the Battle of Plassey and ensuring tactical execution. He later went on to become a key British commander in future campaigns in India. Coote represents the disciplined, career-minded officer class of the East India Company army.

Major Kilpatrick

Clive's subordinate and battlefield adjutant, Major Kilpatrick was involved in both strategic planning and front-line leadership during the Plassey campaign. Known for his grit and loyalty, he helped hold the center line during the battle's most intense moments. His practical outlook often contrasted with Clive's more philosophical reflections.

Mir Madan

Siraj ud-Daulah's most loyal general, Mir Madan was among the few commanders who fought with valor during the Battle of Plassey. He led the main artillery assault and continued to resist even as others hesitated or defected. He died in the field, becoming a tragic symbol of bravery overshadowed by betrayal.

Jagat Seth

A powerful Bengali banker and financier, Jagat Seth played both sides in the lead-up to Plassey. Secretly funding the British and Mir Jafar's conspiracy, he was instrumental in arranging the transfer of power. His role highlights how financial influence often shaped the outcome of political and military conflicts in colonial India.

Miran

The ambitious son of Mir Jafar, Miran quickly began maneuvering for power even as his father's regime faltered under British dominance. Clive saw potential in him as a more pliable future Nawab. His rise marked a shift toward dynastic instability and deepening British control.

.

Postscript: The Thuggee Cult and the Shadow of Clive

Section I: Origins and Practices of the Thuggee

The word "Thuggee" derives from the Hindi *thag*, meaning "swindler" or "deceiver," an apt description of this shadowy cult that haunted the Indian subcontinent for centuries. Unlike ordinary bandits, Thuggees operated under a complex, religiously infused ideology, and their crimes were not driven by simple greed but by a sense of ritual obligation. Their method of murder, typically strangulation using a silk scarf called a *rumāl*, was carried out not in frenzy but with chilling efficiency and spiritual purpose.

The roots of the Thuggee cult are difficult to trace with certainty, but scholars and colonial observers suggest their presence as early as the 13th or 14th century. They may have existed even earlier in more amorphous forms. What distinguishes the Thuggee from other criminal groups is the cohesion of their ritualistic practices and their association with the Hindu goddess Kali, the fierce deity of destruction and rebirth.

According to the Thugs' own mythology, they were divinely ordained to offer human sacrifices to Kali as a means of maintaining cosmic balance. Killing was, to them, an act of devotion.

Unlike cults that retreated from society, the Thuggee were deeply embedded in the rhythms of Indian life. They posed as merchants, pilgrims, or travelers, joining caravans under false pretenses before turning on their unsuspecting companions.

Their victims were typically strangers, which helped avoid vendettas and local repercussions. Before committing a murder, Thugs would perform intricate rituals to determine divine favor. Omens and dreams played a significant role in planning attacks. Once the ritual signs were considered favorable, the Thugs would lure their victims to a predetermined site—

often near a grove or along an isolated road—and strike as a coordinated unit.

The act itself was formulaic: one Thug, often the most experienced, would use the *rumāl* to strangle the victim while another held down the arms. A third might ensure the target remained silent. After the murder, the group would dispose of the body in a previously dug grave or river.

The loot—money, jewelry, or trade goods—was divided according to a strict hierarchy, and part of it was often set aside as a ritual offering. These were not crimes of desperation; they were structured events enacted by men who often viewed themselves as priests fulfilling sacred duty.

The Thuggee did not operate in isolated cells. Instead, they formed extensive networks across regions, sharing coded language, hand signs, and passwords. Membership passed through families, but recruitment could also extend to outsiders. Their organization allowed them to evade detection for centuries. In many villages and towns, local rulers and officials were either complicit in the cult's actions or turned a blind eye, fearing reprisals or benefiting from the spoils.

Colonial estimates suggest that Thuggee murders numbered in the tens of thousands over several centuries. These numbers are debated, often inflated by British sources for propaganda, but even conservative figures suggest a vast and long-lasting epidemic of ritual killing. The British, who prided themselves on order and progress, found in the Thuggee both a challenge to their authority and a justification for deeper intervention.

By the 18th century, as British control in India expanded, encounters with Thuggee networks increased. While British merchants and soldiers were rarely targeted—Thugs preferred anonymity and avoided high-profile cases—the rising presence of the East India Company in interior regions brought increased scrutiny to rural crime. The growing colonial bureaucracy began recording and classifying crimes in a manner India had never seen before. Through this lens of statistical governance, the Thuggee cult, once cloaked in secrecy and oral tradition, began to emerge in colonial awareness as a distinct and sinister phenomenon.

However, the British view of the Thuggee was not merely that of a criminal conspiracy. It was framed as a moral affront to civilization, a symptom of "oriental despotism" and religious perversion. The British position was that Thuggee exemplified everything wrong with India: superstition, lawlessness, and moral depravity. This attitude provided not only a rationale for extermination but a convenient ideological platform from which to justify imperial rule.

Yet, it is important to recognize that the Thuggee thrived not in an anarchic vacuum but within a fragmented political landscape. Prior to British consolidation, India was a patchwork of princely states, tribal regions, and Mughal remnants. Law enforcement was inconsistent, and long-distance travel remained perilous. In this world of decentralized power and shifting loyalties, the Thuggee could move unseen, striking with impunity across borders and provinces.

Their existence also reflects broader themes of marginalization and disenfranchisement. Many Thugs came from lower castes or tribal groups excluded from economic opportunity. In some sense, their cult offered a form of agency and belonging that traditional Indian society denied. Through the ritual of murder, they found identity, purpose, and divine sanction. The Thuggee were not merely killers; they were adherents of a worldview where violence served order, and bloodshed honored gods.

This world, however, was beginning to collapse. As the British East India Company gained dominance, especially after Robert Clive's decisive victory at Plassey in 1757, the reach of colonial authority extended into regions that had once sheltered criminal networks. The Company brought with it not just soldiers and guns, but clerks, tax collectors, and surveyors. Roads were built, trade routes secured, and local rulers either co-opted or displaced. In this tightening web of control, the hidden spaces in which the Thuggee operated began to disappear.

In many ways, the extermination of the Thuggee was a consequence of the same imperial machinery that Clive helped construct. Though Clive himself never encountered the Thuggee directly, his military successes laid the foundation for a colonial regime that would later declare war on the cult. What had once been invisible would soon be exposed, hunted, and dismantled.

Section II: Clive's Conquest and the Infrastructure of Suppression

The defeat of Siraj-ud-Daulah at the Battle of Plassey in 1757 is rightly regarded as a turning point in Indian history. With a modest force of British regulars, European volunteers, and Indian sepoys, Robert Clive orchestrated a decisive victory that effectively transferred control of Bengal—and eventually much of India—into British hands. But Clive's legacy goes beyond military prowess. He built a system of control that laid the foundation for administrative, commercial, and legal structures that would penetrate the Indian subcontinent. It was within this very framework that the eradication of the Thuggee cult would later take place.

Clive's consolidation of Bengal brought with it more than flags and treaties. It brought roads, forts, checkpoints, and a network of Company loyalists who collected taxes, recorded births and deaths, and oversaw local governance. This infrastructure gradually encroached upon regions that had once existed on the periphery of power—regions where Thuggee activity had flourished. The Company's influence extended

outward like a tightening noose, replacing the informal economies and justice systems with codified British law and commercial oversight.

One of the most critical effects of Clive's victory was the stand-
ardization of security and trade. Long-distance travel became
safer, which ironically made Thuggee tactics more conspicu-
ous. In an earlier era, travelers moving through India expected
to encounter danger. Murders and robberies went largely un-
recorded. But under Company rule, particularly with the establishment of waystations and registries, travelers were tracked,
and disappearances became anomalies rather than routine mis-
fortunes. This heightened visibility eroded the

Thuggee's ability to act without scrutiny.

Additionally, Clive and his successors prioritized intelligence
gathering as a cornerstone of governance. Persianized record-
keeping systems were replaced with English and vernacular
documentation. Village elders and local rulers were co-opted
into a bureaucracy that increasingly demanded reports, compli-
ance, and transparency. These measures made it more difficult
for Thuggee operatives to hide in plain sight. Their rituals, once
carried out in hidden groves or beneath the anonymity of night,
began to attract notice.

Moreover, Clive's transformation of the Company into a quasi-
sovereign political authority allowed for sustained military
presence across India. Garrisons were no longer stationed
solely to protect trade routes or fortifications. They became
mobile tools of pacification, able to respond to threats in the
interior. This mobility was key to the later success of anti-
Thuggee campaigns. Sleeman's operations in the 1830s would
have been impossible without the infrastructure of surveillance, roads, and military logistics that Clive had initiated nearly
a century earlier.

Beyond military and administrative reforms, Clive also introduced the foundations of a moral and ideological framework that justified imperial domination. His reports and correspondence often framed Indian rulers as decadent and incapable of good governance. This narrative, while self-serving, would evolve into a central tenet of British colonial ideology: that British rule was a civilizing force. The Thuggee cult—with its rituals, its secrecy, and its devotion to Kali—fit perfectly into this framework as a symbol of Indian barbarism.

The British public back in England devoured stories of Thuggee atrocities with morbid fascination. Newspapers serialized fictionalized Thuggee narratives, painting the cult as a demonic force stalking the innocent. These depictions were not merely entertainment; they served to validate the colonial project. If British officers were ridding India of such savagery, then surely their presence was not only profitable but moral. This perception enabled the British government to support increasingly intrusive measures under the guise of public safety and religious reform.

Thus, Clive's legacy was not just in battles won or forts captured, but in creating a colonial state capable of identifying, isolating, and eradicating threats like the Thuggee. His successors inherited a toolkit of governance—legal codes, maps, administrative posts, intelligence networks, and military logistics—that allowed them to enforce imperial will deep into India's interior. The eradication of the Thuggee was not a single event but the culmination of decades of British expansion, institutionalization, and ideological warfare.

In Section III, we will examine the campaign led by Major-General William Sleeman to destroy the Thuggee cult entirely, and how this campaign marked the symbolic victory of British rationalism over what they viewed as Indian superstition and savagery.

Section III: William Sleeman and the Campaign to Eradicate the Thuggee

By the early 19th century, the infrastructure laid by Clive and his successors had matured into a full-fledged colonial administration. With expanding networks of roads, intelligence, and regional governance, the British had the tools to address longstanding internal threats that earlier regimes could only tolerate or avoid. One such threat was the Thuggee cult, which, despite declining influence, still operated across central and northern India. It was under this backdrop that **Major-General William Henry Sleeman** emerged as the man who would become synonymous with the extermination of the Thuggee.

William Sleeman

Sleeman, a British officer and administrator, was not the first to recognize the threat posed by the Thugs, but he was the first to approach their eradication with methodical, scientific rigor. Prior to his involvement, the British had made sporadic attempts to curb Thuggee activity, but these efforts were hampered by a lack of coordination, inconsistent intelligence, and local resistance. Sleeman changed that. Drawing upon the expanding Company bureaucracy and military presence, he devised a campaign rooted in meticulous record-keeping, native informants, and psychological pressure.

The foundation of Sleeman's success lay in his use of **approvers**—captured Thugs who agreed to cooperate with British authorities in exchange for leniency. These informants provided detailed insights into Thuggee operations: their routes, methods, rituals, and hierarchies. With this information, Sleeman built comprehensive dossiers on suspected Thugs, mapped out their territories, and constructed an intelligence network that extended across multiple provinces.

Sleeman also innovated the use of portable magistrates and mobile police units, allowing for the rapid arrest and interrogation of suspects. His methods were part detective work, part psychological warfare. He exploited rivalries within

Thuggee bands, sowed distrust, and leveraged confessions to turn one member against another. The cumulative effect was to dismantle not just individual cells, but the cultural cohesion and secretiveness that had allowed the cult to thrive.

The campaign against the Thuggee formally began in earnest around 1835 and reached its peak by the early 1840s. During this time, thousands of suspected Thugs were arrested. By Sleeman's own count, over 3,000 individuals were apprehended, with many receiving long sentences, and others executed for their crimes. While some modern historians question the breadth of the operation—and the accuracy of British accounts—there is no doubt that the campaign drastically reduced Thuggee activity.

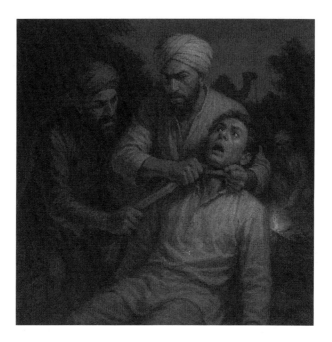

One of Sleeman's great innovations was the creation of a **Thuggee and Dacoity Department**, an intelligence and enforcement agency tasked solely with eliminating ritual criminal activity. The department compiled extensive archives, including personal confessions, family trees, and geographic data, which still survive today as some of the most comprehensive records of criminal investigation from colonial India.

But Sleeman's war on the Thugs was more than just a policing effort—it was a **symbolic victory** for British imperialism.

It represented, in the minds of colonial administrators, the triumph of rational order over mystical chaos, of progress over barbarism. Sleeman was lionized in the British press and celebrated as a civilizing hero. His memoirs and government reports were published and widely read, cementing his place in imperial history.

Yet, the narrative is not without complexity. While the Thuggee cult undoubtedly committed horrific crimes, the British portrayal of them was exaggerated for political purposes. The

Thuggee became a convenient foil—an enemy whose eradication justified intrusive surveillance, legal overreach, and expanded British presence in rural India. Critics both then and now have noted the potential for abuse, including false accusations, coerced confessions, and collective punishment of communities labeled as criminal castes.

Furthermore, the suppression of the Thuggee marked the beginning of a broader pattern in British India: the classification of entire social groups as inherently criminal. This culminated in the **Criminal Tribes Act of 1871**, which institutionalized prejudice against certain castes and communities. In many ways, the British victory over the Thuggee created a dangerous precedent—replacing one form of violence with another, more bureaucratic form of marginalization.

Still, from a historical perspective, Sleeman's campaign stands as one of the most successful law enforcement operations of the early 19th century. It combined intelligence, legal innovation, military support, and psychological insight to dismantle a widespread and deeply rooted criminal cult. And it was only possible because of the colonial architecture that men like

Robert Clive had built decades earlier.

By the end of the 1840s, the Thuggee were no longer a meaningful threat. Their cultic rituals were disbanded, their leaders imprisoned or executed, and their mythology shattered under the weight of colonial documentation. What had once operated in the shadows was now a subject of British classification and control.

In the end, the destruction of the Thuggee was not just a victory of arms or administration. It was a demonstration of how empires create order—not simply through conquest, but through narrative. The British did not merely defeat the

Thugs; they **redefined them**, transforming a covert brotherhood into a symbol of everything the empire claimed to oppose. In doing so, they also justified their own permanence.

Thus, the eradication of the Thuggee cult was not an isolated episode. It was the consequence of an imperial system forged by conquest, solidified through bureaucracy, and sustained by ideology. From the fields of Plassey to the forests of central India, Clive's shadow loomed large. What he began in battle, his successors finished in policy—and the world of the Thuggee vanished beneath the rising tide of empire.

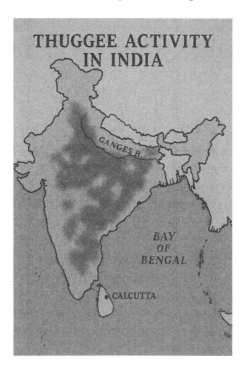

Essay: Shadows of an Empire — Rethinking Colonialism and National Independence in a Modern Age

The legacy of white colonialism remains one of the most contested and consequential chapters in world history. It is both a global narrative of economic expansion and a deeply personal story of racial hierarchy, exploitation, and cultural suppression.

At the heart of this history lies the idea that European powers—predominantly white, Christian, and capitalist—had both the right and duty to control, "civilize," and profit from non-European societies. That belief system, once institutionalized through military conquest and administrative rule, continues to shape our modern world.

In many ways, the struggle between colonialism and national independence is also a struggle between domination and self-definition—between inherited power and earned sovereignty. Understanding this history is not merely academic. It informs how we see global inequality, migration, nationalism, and identity in the 21st century.

Colonialism as a Racial Project

Although economic motives fueled imperial conquest, race was the ideological engine. From the British Raj in India to French Algeria and Belgian Congo, colonizers constructed a hierarchy of civilization in which whiteness became synonymous with progress, order, and modernity. Indigenous peoples were often portrayed as backward, superstitious, and in need of "uplift"—a belief that served to justify both violent subjugation and economic extraction. This was not an incidental part of colonial policy; it was foundational.

Robert Clive's conquest of Bengal in 1757, for example, was not merely a military triumph. It was seen by many in Britain as proof of Anglo-Saxon superiority over "Oriental despotism." The East India Company's control of Indian wealth became a symbol of imperial capability and racial authority. Similarly, colonial officials such as Lord Macaulay argued that English education would create a class of Indian subjects "Indian in blood and color, but English in taste, opinions, and morals." This was a civilizing mission—one rooted in the belief that European culture, religion, and language were inherently superior.

Such ideologies of racial superiority were later exported globally. In Africa, settler colonies like Rhodesia and South Africa entrenched white minority rule. In the Americas, indigenous lands were appropriated under the guise of "manifest destiny." In each case, colonialism depended on a racial logic that dehumanized the colonized and privileged the colonizer.

Resistance and the Birth of National Identity

Yet colonialism did not go unchallenged. In nearly every empire, resistance movements emerged—some violent, others intellectual or spiritual—that sought to reclaim sovereignty and cultural dignity. Figures such as Mahatma Gandhi, Kwame Nkrumah, Ho Chi Minh, and Patrice Lumumba did not merely seek political independence; they sought to dismantle the racial hierarchies imposed by colonialism.

In India, the long struggle for independence fused religious diversity, anti-racist critique, and economic nationalism. Gandhi's concept of *swaraj*, or self-rule, was explicitly opposed to the paternalistic domination of the British. In Algeria, the National Liberation Front (FLN) fought a brutal war not only against French occupation but against the racialized dehumanization that came with it.

Even in cases where decolonization was negotiated peacefully—such as in Ghana or Malaysia—the project of building a post-colonial identity required confronting the legacy of white rule. This included dismantling colonial legal codes, reclaiming indigenous languages, and challenging Eurocentric historical narratives.

In many ways, national independence movements were as much about *psychological* liberation as political autonomy. To assert that colonized people were capable of self-governance was, by definition, to reject the racial logic of colonialism.

Post-Colonial Challenges and Neo-Colonial Realities

However, national independence did not always result in immediate empowerment. Many former colonies inherited economies structured around export dependency, education systems that marginalized local knowledge, and political borders drawn arbitrarily by imperial cartographers. These structural hangovers—often called "neo-colonialism"—meant that formal sovereignty coexisted with continued economic and cultural subordination.

Moreover, white supremacy as a global ideology did not dissolve with decolonization. International financial institutions, global media, and even humanitarian aid often carried forward implicit racial assumptions about governance, development, and worthiness. Former colonial powers continued to exert influence over their ex-colonies through military alliances, trade dependencies, and corporate investment.

In this context, the racial legacy of colonialism became more diffuse but no less real. Disparities in global health, wealth, and education frequently reflect the boundaries drawn—and minds shaped—by centuries of colonial rule. And in the diaspora, people of formerly colonized nations often face racial discrimination in the very countries that once claimed to govern them.

Global Capital and the Persistence of Neo-Colonialism

The structures of colonialism may have been formally disman-tled, but their economic architecture remains firmly in place. Today, many former colonies continue to operate within global trade systems designed during the imperial era. Multinational corporations—often headquartered in former colonial capi-tals—extract raw materials, enforce patent monopolies, and shape local labor markets to their advantage.

These economic imbalances echo the days when Britain si-phoned Bengal's wealth or France controlled West African rail-ways and rubber plantations.

In places like Nigeria, India, and Indonesia, the state often re-mains constrained by international debt obligations and free-market reforms imposed by the International Monetary Fund and World Bank. These institutions, while nominally neutral, often promote neoliberal policies that privilege foreign inves-tors over domestic welfare. This can result in reduced public services, weakened labor protections, and environmental deg-radation.

Moreover, corporate globalization often replicates colonial hi-erarchies. Companies extract minerals from the Democratic Republic of Congo using local labor under dangerous condi-tions, while profits accrue in European or North American bank accounts. The smartphone industry, for instance, relies on cobalt mined under conditions not far removed from forced labor. While empires are gone, the pipelines of exploi-tation remain.

Comparative Struggles: Africa and Asia in the Shadow of Empire

Although each national independence movement had unique contours, they shared common strategies and common ene-mies. Across Africa and Asia, resistance to white colonialism was both an assertion of national dignity and a direct rejection of racial hierarchy.

In Kenya, the Mau Mau uprising represented a grassroots armed struggle against British settler colonialism and land dispossession. Though brutally suppressed, it galvanized nationalist sentiment and paved the way for independence in 1963.

Similarly, Vietnam's long war of liberation—first against the French, then the United States—was as much about racial sovereignty as it was about geopolitics.

In Ghana, Kwame Nkrumah combined pan-African ideals with Marxist thought to imagine a future where African nations could stand united against Western economic dependency. His vision of a decolonized, federated Africa inspired generations, even if it was cut short by internal and external pressures. In South Africa, the anti-apartheid movement stood as a prolonged and painful confrontation with a racialized form of colonial rule that claimed legal legitimacy well into the 1990s.

These movements underscore that the fight for national independence was rarely limited to political autonomy. It was about cultural revival, social transformation, and reclaiming agency from centuries of racial domination.

Decolonizing the Mind: Education, Culture, and Historical Truth

One of the most insidious legacies of white colonialism is the control of historical memory. Colonized peoples were often taught to revere their conquerors and internalize their own supposed inferiority. British schools in India taught Shakespeare and Newton, but little about Kalidasa or Aryabhata. In African colonies, European history was prioritized while pre-colonial African civilizations were dismissed as primitive or irrelevant.

Decolonizing education is not simply about replacing one curriculum with another—it's about shifting the framework of knowledge itself. It means questioning whose voices are heard, whose histories are prioritized, and what kinds of intelligence are validated. It also means elevating indigenous knowledge systems, oral traditions, and languages that were once deliberately suppressed.

The return of cultural artifacts—such as the Benin Bronzes from British museums or temple idols looted during Company campaigns—is part of this process. These objects are not just art; they are vessels of memory and meaning. Their restitution is an acknowledgment that colonialism was not just political—it was cultural theft.

In universities and classrooms worldwide, there is now a growing effort to teach empire not as a benign spread of civilization, but as a violent, racialized system that shaped modern inequality. The aim is not to induce guilt, but to encourage understanding—and from that understanding, justice.

Rethinking Independence in the 21st Century

What, then, does national independence mean in a globalized world still shaped by colonial patterns?

On one hand, former colonies have made tremendous strides—electing their own leaders, building new institutions, and contributing richly to global culture and innovation. On the other, many continue to wrestle with internal divisions, underdevelopment, and dependence on Western economic structures.

True independence, in this context, must include cultural and epistemological sovereignty—the right to define one's history, identity, and future outside of colonial frames. It also requires accountability from former colonizers—not merely symbolic apologies, but meaningful engagement with the material and psychological debts of empire.

This may include reparations, land reform, educational reform, or the return of stolen cultural artifacts. But more fundamentally, it requires a commitment to equity—not just in politics, but in imagination.

Conclusion: From Empire to Equity

The racial legacy of white colonialism cannot be undone overnight. But it can be confronted. It can be named. And it can be resisted through acts of historical clarity, cultural affirmation, and international solidarity.

Robert Clive may have stood atop the battlefield at Plassey as the harbinger of empire. But the story did not end there. From the jungles of India to the streets of Johannesburg, from Caribbean plantations to Polynesian outposts, colonized peoples have spoken back. They have written poems, passed laws, staged uprisings, and dreamed new nations into being.

In that sense, national independence is not a date on a calendar. It is an ongoing process—a daily rejection of the notion that whiteness is destiny, and a collective assertion that dignity belongs to all.

History remembers the conquerors. But the future belongs to the liberated.

Final Essay: From Plassey to Rebellion: The Roots of the Sepoy Mutiny in the Battle of Plassey

The Battle of Plassey in 1757 marked a turning point in the history of India. It was not just a military engagement but a profound moment of imperial transition, shifting power from indigenous rulers to a foreign commercial enterprise—the British East India Company. Precisely one hundred years later, in 1857, India erupted in widespread revolt during what has come to be known as the Sepoy Rebellion, or the First War of Indian Independence.

While separated by a century, the two events are tightly interwoven in cause and consequence. The seeds of 1857 were sown in the muddy fields of Bengal, where Robert Clive's victory at Plassey transformed a trading company into a colonial power. This essay examines how the mechanisms of control established after Plassey, the exploitation and transformation of Indian society under Company rule, and the militarization of Indian soldiers (sepoys) led inexorably to the rebellion of 1857.

I. The Battle of Plassey: The Beginning of British Political Control

The Battle of Plassey, fought on June 23, 1757, was a relatively small engagement between the forces of the British East India Company under Robert Clive and the army of Siraj-ud-Daulah, the Nawab of Bengal. Despite being outnumbered, the British triumphed due to a combination of bribery, treachery, and superior artillery. Key figures in the Nawab's camp, particularly Mir Jafar, defected to the British side in return for promises of power and wealth.

Though it lasted only a few hours, the victory gave the British control over Bengal, the richest province in India. More than a battlefield success, it represented a paradigm shift: the East India Company became not merely a commercial entity but a political power, administering vast territories and collecting taxes. The extraction of wealth from Bengal began in earnest after Plassey, funding Britain's industrial revolution while impoverishing Indian society.

The implications of Plassey were immense:
- The British East India Company acquired de facto sovereignty, starting with Bengal and slowly extending across India.
- Local rulers and systems of governance were subordinated to Company authority.
- Indian soldiers began to be employed in large numbers to protect Company interests—a precursor to the sepoy armies.

This shift in governance laid the foundation for colonial exploitation, systemic racism, and cultural erosion—all of which would ferment rebellion a century later.

II. The Establishment of Company Rule and Its Effects on Indian Society

Post-Plassey, the British East India Company adopted a governance model that maximized revenue extraction while minimizing direct administrative investment. In 1765, after the Battle of Buxar, the Diwani rights (right to collect revenue) of Bengal, Bihar, and Orissa were granted to the Company by the Mughal Emperor Shah Alam II. This transformed the Company from a trading power into a de facto sovereign.

Revenue collection practices became increasingly exploitative:

- Traditional Indian landlords (zamindars) were co-opted or replaced by those loyal to British interests.
- Agricultural practices were distorted to serve British industries—for example, the forced cultivation of indigo and opium.
- The Permanent Settlement Act of 1793 created a class of absentee landlords, leading to widespread peasant poverty.

The wealth siphoned from Bengal and other provinces did not benefit the Indian population. Famines, such as the Bengal Famine of 1770, were exacerbated by British indifference or economic mismanagement.

Culturally, Company rule introduced Western education, law, and social reforms, which—while well-intentioned in some cases—often eroded traditional Indian values and institutions. The introduction of English-language education and Christian missionary activities was perceived by many Indians as an assault on their religion and way of life.

III. The Rise of the Sepoy Army

To maintain their expanding dominion, the British relied heavily on Indian soldiers, or sepoys, who were recruited from diverse ethnic and religious backgrounds. These sepoys became the backbone of the Company's military power.

The conditions of sepoy service became increasingly restrictive and degrading:
- Sepoys were paid low wages, often delayed or docked.
- Promotion was largely restricted to British officers, regardless of sepoy merit.
- In some cases, sepoys were ordered to serve in regions that violated their caste or religious customs.

Over time, sepoys grew disillusioned with their treatment. They saw themselves not as servants of a foreign power but as rightful protectors of their homeland. The Company, however, viewed them as tools of empire.

One of the most telling ironies of British colonialism is that the same Indian soldiers who enabled the expansion of British power would one day be its greatest threat. Without the sepoys' loyalty, the empire would crumble.

IV. Seeds of Discontent: Political, Economic, and Religious Grievances

By the early 19th century, unrest was spreading. While the military structure of Company rule held firm, the social and religious fabric of India was fraying.

Political Discontent

The annexation policies of the Governor-General Lord Dalhousie, especially the Doctrine of Lapse, angered Indian rulers and elites. Under this policy, any princely state without a biological male heir was annexed by the Company. This led to the seizure of prominent territories like Satara, Jhansi, and Awadh (Oudh).

The annexation of Oudh in 1856 was particularly inflammatory:

- It displaced many noble families.
- It disbanded local armies, creating thousands of unemployed, armed men.
- The sepoy army drew heavily from Oudh, making it a direct insult to many soldiers.

Economic Discontent

As the British imposed their economic model, traditional artisans, weavers, and farmers suffered:

- Indian textile industries collapsed under the weight of imported British goods.

- Artisans became beggars; famines increased.
- The imposition of taxes on local goods and the destruction of domestic industry created deep economic grievances.

Religious and Cultural Discontent

The perception that the British were attempting to Christianize India became widespread:
- Missionaries were active in schools and the military.
- New laws, such as permitting the remarriage of Hindu widows, were seen as attacks on Hindu dharma.
- The introduction of the Enfield rifle, which required sepoys to bite off cartridges allegedly greased with cow and pig fat, was the final spark. To Hindus, the cow is sacred; to Muslims, the pig is unclean.

This act, whether intentional or not, symbolized the deeper colonial disrespect for Indian religious values.

V. The Sepoy Rebellion of 1857: A Century in the Making

The rebellion began in Meerut in May 1857, when sepoys who refused to use the Enfield cartridges were imprisoned.

Fellow soldiers rose up, killing their British officers and marching to Delhi, where they declared the aged Mughal emperor Bahadur Shah Zafar the symbolic leader of the revolt.
The rebellion spread like wildfire across North and Central India—Kanpur, Lucknow, Jhansi, Gwalior—driven by shared grievances:
- Sepoys felt betrayed and disrespected.
- Rulers and nobles resented annexation and loss of prestige.
- Common people had suffered under economic exploitation and cultural marginalization.

Though initially successful in some regions, the rebellion lacked coordination and clear leadership. The British eventually suppressed it with brutal force, often massacring entire populations as retribution.

But the rebellion changed everything.

VI. The Legacy: Connecting Plassey to 1857

The Battle of Plassey and the Sepoy Rebellion were bookends of the Company Raj. Plassey represented the beginning of British dominance, while 1857 marked its collapse in legitimacy.

Key Connections
1. Militarization of India: Plassey inaugurated the use of Indian troops in British service, a system that eventually backfired.
2. Economic Exploitation: The wealth extracted post-Plassey destabilized Indian agriculture and industry, creating misery that would later fuel rebellion.
3. Political Dispossession: British expansionism, rooted in Plassey's victory, systematically eroded Indian sovereignty.
4. Cultural Alienation: The arrogance of power gained at Plassey fostered a colonial mindset that dismissed Indian customs—provoking outrage over time.

In many ways, the rebellion of 1857 was the natural consequence of the policies initiated after Plassey. A system based on betrayal, profit, and coercion was inherently unstable.

Conclusion

The road from Plassey to the Sepoy Rebellion was not merely a chronological path—it was a moral and political arc that revealed the dangers of unchecked imperialism. What began as a business venture in 1757 had, by 1857, transformed into a colonial machine sustained by violence, injustice, and cultural contempt.

The sepoys who rose in revolt were not just mutineers reacting to greased cartridges. They were the product of a hundred years of subjugation, born in the shadow of Robert Clive's opportunistic coup at Plassey. Their rebellion, though ultimately unsuccessful, forced the British Crown to reassess its governance. In the aftermath, the British East India Company was dissolved, and India came under direct Crown rule, ushering in a new era of imperialism—but also planting the seeds for India's eventual independence.

In this light, Plassey and 1857 are not two isolated events but chapters of a single story—a century of colonization, resistance, and the enduring desire of a people to reclaim their destiny.

Pop Culture References to the Battle of Plassey

ROBERT CLIVE AND THE BATTLE OF PLASSEY in POPULAR CULTURE

BOOKS	MOVIES / TV	TOYS / VIDEO GAMES
The Anarchy by William Dalrymple	• Clive of India (1935)	• Age of Empires III: *The Asian Dynasties*
Clive of India by Nirad C. Chaudhuri	• Bharat Ek Khoj (1988)	• Empire: Total War
Clive: *The Life and Death of a British Emperor* by Robert Harvey	• The Story of India (2007)	• Assassin's Creed Chronicles: *India*
White Mughals by William Dalrymple	• Empire (2005)	• Sid Meier's Civilization VI (Expansion Packs)
The Honourable Company by John Keay	• The Anarchy (*upcoming adapiation*)	• Liberty or Death
Flashman in the Great Game by George MacDonald Fraser		
The Discovery of India by Jauaharlal Nehru		

Teacher's Guide: The Time of Clive

Overview: *The Time of Clive* is a cinematic historical novel tracing the rise of Robert Clive and the events leading to the Battle of Plassey in 1757, which launched the British East India Company into imperial power across the Indian subcontinent. With a narrative driven by action, betrayal, and real-world political consequences, the book explores colonial ambition, native resistance, and the ethical complexities of empire.

Grade Level: 10th Grade and Up
Subject Areas: History, World Cultures, Literature, Ethics, Post-Colonial Studies

Objectives:
- Analyze the causes and consequences of the Battle of Plassey.
- Understand the structure and influence of the British East India Company.
- Explore the role of individual agency in historical change.
- Compare British and Indian perspectives on colonialism.
- Develop critical thinking about empire, economic exploitation, and historical memory.

Key Themes:
- Colonialism and its legacy
- Betrayal and political intrigue
- The role of private enterprise in warfare
- Cultural misunderstanding and imperial ideology
- Leadership, power, and responsibility

Reading Schedule (Suggested):
Week 1: Prologue + Chapters 1–4 – Clive's Early Life and Voyage to India

Week 2: Chapters 5–9 – The East India Company and the Road   to   War
Week 3: Chapters 10–17 – The Battle of Plassey (Expanded)
Week 4: Chapters 18–19 + Epilogue – Aftermath, Legacy, and Reflections

Discussion Questions:
1. How does Robert Clive change throughout the novel, and what internal conflicts does he face?
2. What were the economic motivations behind British involvement in Bengal?
3. How did Indian actors like Siraj ud-Daulah, Mir Jafar, and Jagat Seth shape the outcome of the battle?
4. Was the East India Company a government, a corporation, or something else?
5. How is the legacy of Plassey still felt today?
6. What are the ethical implications of Clive's choices? Can ambition be separated from morality in war?
7. How does the novel balance historical accuracy with narrative drama?

In-Class Activities:
- Primary Source Comparison: Analyze excerpts from Clive's real correspondence and compare with fictionalized dialogue.
- Debate: Should Clive be remembered as a hero, a villain, or something in between?
- Map Exercise: Plot the major locations mentioned in the novel (Calcutta, Plassey, Murshidabad, etc.) and trace military movements.
- Historical vs. Literary: Examine scenes that deviate from known history. Why might the author have taken these liberties?

Extension Assignments:
- Essay: How did the Battle of Plassey alter the global balance of power in the 18th century?

- Creative Writing: Write a first-person account of the battle from the perspective of a sepoy or Bengali villager.
- Research Project: Investigate the 1770 Bengal famine and its roots in Company policy.
- Art/Design: Create a propaganda poster or Company recruitment ad as it might have appeared in 1757.

Assessment:
- Participation in discussion and activities
- Weekly reading quizzes
- Final essay or creative project
- Historical context presentation

Further Reading / Resources:
- *The Anarchy* by William Dalrymple
- *The Discovery of India* by Jawaharlal Nehru (excerpts)
- *The Corporation That Changed the World* by Nick Robins
- *India: A History* by John Keay
- Primary documents from the British East India Company archives

Note to Educators:
This book blends fiction and fact. Encourage students to research the actual historical figures and cross-reference with the narrative. The aim is not just to learn what happened but to think critically about how and why we tell stories about empire—and who gets to tell them.

Author's Final Note: Modern Perspectives on Plassey

History must always be judged within the context of its time. The figures, actions, and empires we explore in these pages were shaped by the norms, ambitions, and blind spots of their era. Yet even with that understanding, some truths echo louder through time.

By modern standards, there can be little doubt: the Battle of Plassey was, in many ways, the first battle for Indian independence.

It was not a government, nor a sovereign nation, that seized Bengal—but a corporation. The East India Company, a private commercial entity with its own army and profit motives, conquered by force. It was a takeover not by flag or faith, but by ledger and sword. And from that moment forward, India was never the same.

Just as the Zulu Wars have come to be recognized not merely as colonial campaigns but as one of the most heroic last stands of an indigenous people, so too should we view Plassey through a dual lens.

While this book was written from a Western perspective and focuses primarily on Robert Clive, that lens is not intended to obscure or diminish the vital importance of seeing this event through Indian eyes. Siraj ud-Daulah, Mir Madan, and the countless unnamed soldiers who resisted foreign domination deserve remembrance not as footnotes, but as central players, if not heroes and martyrs, in the story of Indian colonial resistance.

My decision to focus on Clive was a creative one, born—like many obsessions—of childhood. As noted in the introduction, it was a cinematic fascination, not a political one. That said, no single viewpoint can ever tell the whole story. And no telling of Plassey should be considered complete without listening to the voices of those whose land, lives, and legacies were forever changed.

There is a rich and growing library of work on the Battle of Plassey—accounts written from both sides of the battlefield. I strongly encourage readers to explore the Suggested Reading section below, and to engage with the history of India not as a monologue, but as a dialogue.

All stories deserve to be told.*

And all voices deserve to be heard.
— *Scott Neitlich*
Greensboro, NC 2025.

Except the story of the Giant Rat of Sumatra. The world is not yet ready for that tale.

References and Further Reading:

Ali, Daud. 2011. *Courtly Culture and Political Life in Early Medieval India*. Cambridge University Press.
Andrews, Charles Freer. 1937. *The Renaissance in India*. George Allen & Unwin.

Bayly, C. A. 1983. *Rulers, Townsmen and Bazaars: North Indian Society in the Age of British Expansion, 1770–1870*. Cambridge University Press.

Bayly, C. A. 2004. *The Birth of the Modern World, 1780–1914: Global Connections and Comparisons*. Wiley-Blackwell.

Bhattacharya, Neeladri. 2019. *The Great Agrarian Conquest: The Colonial Reshaping of a Rural World*. SUNY Press.

Bose, Sugata, and Ayesha Jalal. 2017. *Modern South Asia: History, Culture, Political Economy*. 4th ed. Routledge.

Bowen, H. V. 2006. *The Business of Empire: The East India Company and Imperial Britain, 1756–1833*. Cambridge University Press.

Bryant, G. J. 2013. *The Emergence of British Power in India, 1600–1784: A Grand Strategic Interpretation*. Boydell & Brewer.

Chakrabarty, Dipesh. 2009. *Provincializing Europe: Postcolonial Thought and Historical Difference*. Princeton University Press.

Chatterjee, Partha. 1993. *The Nation and Its Fragments: Colonial and Postcolonial Histories*. Princeton University Press.

Chaudhuri, K. N. 1978. *The Trading World of Asia and the English East India Company, 1660–1760*. Cambridge University Press.
Chopra, P. N. 2002. *A Comprehensive History of India*. Sterling Publishers.

Dalrymple, William. 2002. *White Mughals: Love and Betrayal in Eighteenth-Century India*. Penguin Books.

Dalrymple, William. 2019. *The Anarchy: The East India Company, Corporate Violence, and the Pillage of an Empire*. Bloomsbury Publishing.

Dirks, Nicholas B. 2006. *The Scandal of Empire: India and the Creation of Imperial Britain*. Harvard University Press.

Ferguson, Niall. 2003. *Empire: The Rise and Demise of the British World Order and the Lessons for Global Power*. Basic Books.

Fisher, Michael H. 1993. *The Politics of the British Annexation of India, 1757–1857*. Oxford University Press.

Fisher, Michael H. 2007. *A Short History of the Mughal Empire*. I.B. Tauris.

Ghosh, Durba. 2006. *Sex and the Family in Colonial India: The Making of Empire*. Cambridge University Press.

Gilmour, David. 2005. *The Ruling Caste: Imperial Lives in the Victorian Raj*. Farrar, Straus and Giroux.

Gommans, Jos. 2017. *The Indian Frontier: Horse and Warband in the Making of Empires*. Routledge.

Guha, Ranajit. 1982. *Dominance without Hegemony: History and Power in Colonial India*. Harvard University Press.

Guha, Ranajit, ed. 1987. *Subaltern Studies V: Writings on South Asian History and Society*. Oxford University Press.
Habib, Irfan. 1999. *The Agrarian System of Mughal India: 1556–1707*. Oxford University Press.

Havinden, Michael, and David Meredith. 2002. *Colonialism and Development: Britain and Its Tropical Colonies, 1850–1960.* Routledge.

Hibbert, Christopher. *The Great Mutiny: India, 1857.* New York: Viking Press, 1978.

James, Lawrence. 1997. *Raj: The Making and Unmaking of British India.* St. Martin's Press.

Jasanoff, Maya. 2005. *Edge of Empire: Lives, Culture, and Conquest in the East, 1750–1850.* Vintage.
Jenkins, Roy. 2001. *Churchill: A Biography.* Macmillan.

Keay, John. 2001. *India: A History.* Grove Press.

Keay, John. 1991. *The Honourable Company: A History of the English East India Company.* HarperCollins.

Kerr, Ian. 2001. *Engines of Change: The Railroads That Made India.* Praeger.

Marshall, P. J. 2005. *The Making and Unmaking of Empires: Britain, India, and America c. 1750–1783.* Oxford University Press.

Marshall, P. J., ed. 1997. *The Eighteenth Century in Indian History: Evolution or Revolution?* Oxford University Press.

Metcalf, Barbara D., and Thomas R. Metcalf. 2006. *A Concise History of Modern India.* 2nd ed. Cambridge University Press.

Misra, B. B. 1959. *The Central Administration of the East India Company, 1773–1834.* Manchester University Press.

Mukherjee, Rudrangshu. 2002. *Awadh in Revolt, 1857–1858: A Study of Popular Resistance.* Permanent Black.

Nehru, Jawaharlal. 1946. *The Discovery of India.* Oxford University Press.

Parsons, Timothy H. 2004. *The British Imperial Century, 1815–1914: A World History Perspective.* Rowman & Littlefield.

Riddick, John F. 2006. *The History of British India: A Chronology.* Greenwood Press.

Robins, Nick. 2006. *The Corporation That Changed the World: How the East India Company Shaped the Modern Multinational.* Pluto Press.

Roy, Tirthankar. 2011. *The East India Company: The World's Most Powerful Corporation.* Allen Lane.

Said, Edward W. 1978. *Orientalism.* Pantheon Books.

Sen, Sudipta. 1998. *Empire of Free Trade: The East India Company and the Making of the Colonial Marketplace.* University of Pennsylvania Press.

Spears, Major-General Edward. 1930. *The Wars of the East India Company.* Clarendon Press.
Stokes, Eric. 1973. *The English Utilitarians and India.* Oxford University Press.

Wilson, Jon E. 2016. *India Conquered: Britain's Raj and the Chaos of Empire.* Simon & Schuster.

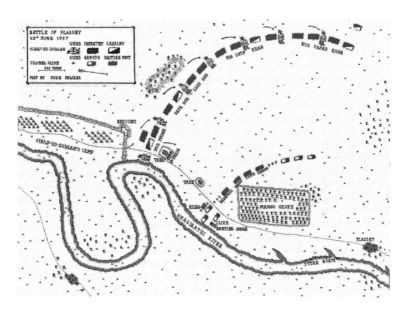

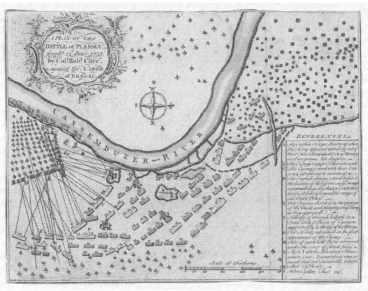

Scott Neitlich is a writer, historian, and lifelong explorer of forgotten stories. In addition to his published work, he also runs the highly popular YouTube channel *Spector Creative* offering insights into pop culture, history and media.

He holds an BA from UCSB and an MBA from UNCG.
He lives in Greensboro, North Carolina with his wife, daughter and 10,000 books.

Also available:

Made in the USA
Columbia, SC
21 May 2025

58128141R00135